7/27/12

D1648854

To Janet:

Be Bold!

☺

Content Marketing Institute books are available at special quantity discounts to use as premiums and sales promotions, or for use in corporate training programs. To place a bulk order, please contact the Content Marketing Institute at info@contentinstitute.com or 888/554-2014.

ISBN 978-0-9833307-4-5

Printed in the United States of America.

BOLD
BRAND

The new rules for differentiating, branding, and marketing your professional services firm.

Josh Miles

Foreword by Mark Zweig

To April, my best friend, my bride, and my inspiration.

To Meg and Griffin, may you always follow your dreams.

To Mom, Dad, and my teachers for your guidance.

To our clients for making my passion a career.

Table of contents:

It's time to shake things up.

Foreword

I'm Mark Zweig. As the founder and CEO of ZweigWhite, a twice-named Inc. 500 consulting, publishing, training, and media firm dedicated to serving the A/E and environmental consulting industry, I have worked with literally thousands of firms over the last 32 years. And you know what? The majority of them are horrible marketers who have no clue about how to differentiate themselves in a (very) crowded market by creating a brand.

Those firms that do "get" this idea usually become wildly successful. They are the fast-growth firms, the mega firms, the "hot" firms, and the firms that make the most money. They are also the firms that have all their peers and competitors wondering how they get such high billing rates or why they are so successful when they "really aren't very good designers." I have seen this so many times you wouldn't believe it!

The typical professional services firm doesn't really believe in the power of brand building. They think that only applies to laundry detergent or toothpaste or product makers like Apple. They see no parallel with the story of "Geek Squad" and how it came from nowhere in a few short years to completely dominate a fragmented industry like computer repair and network consulting.

Whenever I introduce the topic of brand building during a board meeting or in the course of a business planning consulting project, most professional services firm principals reply with one or more of these statements:

"It (brand building) doesn't apply to us."

"We are professionals—we aren't selling a product."

"Marketing in our business is all about who you know."

"We see marketing as an overhead expense. Overhead is bad and we seek to minimize it."

"We believe in word-of-mouth advertising." (That means we don't do ANY advertising!)

"We don't spend any time on marketing. We SELL!"

Most firms in this business want to spend what the other guy does on marketing and do the same things the other guys do. So guess what happens? They all pretty much do about as well as the other guy—and rise and fall collectively based on the condition of the economy or the submarkets they provide services to.

That's why it's time to shake things up. Josh Miles' book, Bold Brand, does just that. He has the stories, the examples, the process, and the know-how to show anyone where their thinking has gone amiss and how to steal some plays from the playbook of the best brand-building companies anywhere to help make your firm a brand name. His framework walks professional services firms through the right steps to really stand out and do a most difficult job—differentiate their firms from the other guys!

Because the fact is, that when you stop relying on personal selling and personal relationships to get work and instead build a brand that makes the phone ring and the emails pour in, THAT is when you have created a business that may let you exit some day—and one that will be able to survive the comings and goings of just about anyone. When you have a brand, the economy can rise and fall and you will not only survive it, but also keep doing better and better every year.

And what about value in the end? What kind of a firm do you think is more marketable—one that has all its marketing success tied to the efforts of one or a few key people, or one that has a brand name so strong that clients want them even if they don't know WHO from the firm will do their project?

So stop reading this and get on with the book. It's never too early—or too late—to work on your brand. And the rewards are so rich for doing so!

Mark C. Zweig
Founder & CEO
ZweigWhite, LLC

Principal Owner
Mark Zweig, Inc.

Executive-in-Residence
Sam M. Walton College of Business
University of Arkansas

EVENTS

MEALS

NETWORKING

GOLF OUTINGS

YELLOW PAGES

CHAPTER ONE

Where Are All of the Professional Services Brands?

A brief history of professional services marketing and why the old ways are no longer enough.

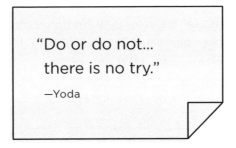

"Do or do not...
there is no try."

—Yoda

Historically speaking, marketing activity in professional services firms can be summed up in one word: relationships. So if most professionals build their practices on relationships, why is the model changing? Why are so many firms resisting new ways of building their brands and marketing their services?

Why professional services brands need help.

According to recent studies, there are more than 1 million professional services businesses in the United States alone. These attorneys, architects, engineers, accountants, business coaches, and other consultants are among the most highly skilled and sought-after professionals in the world. And until recently, having a large ad in the phone book, attending benefit dinners, networking, golfing, wining and dining, and having a brochure-style website were the only types of marketing activities any of these professional firms needed to do.

At the same time, billions of dollars are being spent worldwide to market business-to-consumer (B2C) products and services. The goal? To create and leverage unique and memorable brands.

Historically, business-to-business (B2B) brand development and marketing has been perceived as an incredibly different, less interesting undertaking than B2C marketing.

Today, professional services marketers are waking up.

With the prevalence of web-based technologies and social media, consumers and businesses alike are doing more and more business over the web. But when we look at social media, that's different than branding or marketing, right? Where does one end and the other begin, especially in the context of a professional services business?

Brand is the sum of everything you are.

In his groundbreaking book, *The Brand Gap: How to Bridge the Distance Between Business Strategy and Design*, Marty Neumeier defines brand as "the sum of everything you are." Neumeier says your brand is "not what you say it is, it's what THEY say it is." His overarching argument is that a chasm exists between logic and magic in most organizations. He says that a greater focus on brand could close that gap and generate even greater success for an organization.

I couldn't agree more.

However, we have clients and colleagues with years of marketing or design experience who remain fuzzy on how to grow or influence the development of a brand. Somehow the idea that "it's what THEY say it is" feels like a reason not to try to improve the brand. If the brand is created only in the minds of consumers, somehow the very exercise of "branding" seems less than forthright—like trickery or intentionally trying to mislead the consumer.

We believe your brand encompasses every element of your organization. It's in the delivery of your product or service, your office space, your building, your visual identity...your use of language, signature sounds, and images...and just as importantly, your user experience, policies, customer service, and the conversations being had about you. In short, it's everything from your physical existence to your reputation.

So if brand is EVERYTHING that surrounds your organization, what good is branding?

It's important to remember that much of a brand is somewhat passive. We can't possibly control or influence the conversations employees have about our company on the weekends, or the reputation we have for poor customer service, right? WRONG.

Branding certainly can't take a lousy company and help it look like a great one. However, focusing on what needs improvement in an organization from the ground-up and the inside-out, and repackaging the organization in a new light can successfully and completely recreate the public image of that brand. That's why they call it a rebrand.

Your brand is like a living, breathing, malleable, and pliable entity. It's greatly influenced by intentional positioning and differentiating your firm, but is also responsive to the feedback of your clients and customers. It's the thing that allows you to charge a premium for the same services your competition offers.

Brand is what keeps your firm not only top-of-mind in the marketplace, but also preferred.

Why are professional services brands so far behind?

As world-renowned sales trainer Zig Ziglar once said, "People buy from people." So it stands to reason, if branding B2C products and services is a worthy endeavor, then why have B2B products—and specifically the highly sought after expertise of professional services firms—been so overlooked by marketers, branding and design companies, and firm leadership?

I have two theories.

My first theory is that working for better-known, sexier B2C clients such as consumer packaged goods, automobile manufacturers, and sports franchises seems more exciting.

My second theory is that the professionals who run these firms—as well as most of the marketers who try to serve them—don't even know where to begin.

Developing a unique brand for a professional services firm is a collaborative effort, often between multiple partners within a firm, various stakeholders, and an entire practice often categorized by a high degree of intellectual capacity. Building a great brand from these conditions is no simple task. That's why in today's marketplace, you're more likely to find professional "bland brands"—a collection of undifferentiated, me-too brands that do things just the way they always have.

Where can we find evidence of these professional services "bland brands"? One obvious place to start is the web. Most professional services firms look to their website or even to their social media presence to take care of their branding needs. Unfortunately, the roots of their marketing problems are not in the quality of their website or social media programs. The root problem is the absence of an overarching, holistic brand strategy, as well as a failure to find, leverage, and express the most distinguishing elements of their brand.

It's time to ditch your bland brand and create a Bold Brand™.

Bold Brand™ is a framework and best-practices approach designed to help professional services firms identify a niche, position themselves within that niche, and build a compelling brand. This framework guides professionals step-by-step through the process, illuminating potential pitfalls along the way.

As varied as professional services firms may be from each other, why on earth would they benefit from operating from the same branding framework? It's as simple as knowing where to begin, what to build from, and which elements of your branding and marketing can and should evolve over time. In today's online marketplace, even brilliant professionals can quickly waste energy and resources on the wrong tactics at the wrong times. As new social networks, mobile, cloud-based apps, and other new media quickly emerge as the latest-and-greatest marketing channels, professional services firms are left wondering if these approaches are where their marketing dollars should be spent today, if at all.

Behind closed doors:
the questions about "brands."

In talking with business owners, partners, and marketing professionals, I hear similar problems and concerns over and over again. I've heard questions about the permanence of social media. I've listened to stories about the challenges of standing out in a crowded marketplace. I've heard tales about companies growing out of control, with no consistent way of sharing their culture with new employees. And I've heard the frustration of bringing an unmatched service to market, only to have to compete on price against dozens of lesser-qualified, me-too companies.

But the most interesting questions are the ones I hear behind closed doors—the whispered questions that people ask once we've developed a deeper level of trust. These are the types of things I hear nearly every week from business owners, partners, and marketers of professional services:

> "Branding? Marketing? Website? How do we know what to tackle first? All I know is we need to drive sales."

> "We're experts in this market, but we're always competing against these lower-tier competitors. Nobody seems to understand that comparing us to the rest of the marketplace just isn't 'apples to apples.' And so often the decision comes down to which vendor is the cheapest. How do we convince them we're the experts?"

> "Sure, I think strategy is important, but isn't social media what everyone else is focusing on right now?"

> "As the vice president of sales and marketing, I may have 'marketing' in my title, but I don't know anything about that creative stuff. That's why we need you guys... Does that

stuff really work?"

"We don't need branding. We already have a brand. All of our clients know who we are, and all of our sales are from our relationships."

"I don't know the difference between marketing and advertising. Should we budget for them separately?"

"I don't think we're going to do any 'branding' ads. We've tried that before and they're a waste of money."

"Our niece designed our logo (gesturing to the sign on the wall) … it's a little difficult to reproduce in color, but we don't want to change it anytime soon. She'd be devastated."

"We spent a lot of money on that sign out front. It's just not worth rebranding if we have to replace that. Signs are expensive."

"All we need is to make our website look more up-to-date. We can give you the stock photos and the shot of our building. We'll show you where to put everything. That should be pretty straightforward, right?"

"We can address our brand strategy later. For now, we have to get more leads through our website."

"Okay, you've been talking a lot through this process about 'branding.' What exactly do you mean by this whole 'brand' thing?"

Do any of these questions sound familiar? As I mentioned, they're very common. In fact, in the professional services space, this disconnect between the power of a brand and its connection to the bottom line is nearly the rule.

Not all of the people asking these questions are in a sales or marketing position, per se. Few of them have much experience in building a brand, let alone any formal training in design, branding, or marketing. Sometimes the MBAs and others who do have marketing training are even more difficult to deal with. Many MBAs understand the book definitions, but lack the real-world experience of actually 'doing marketing.' I once had an MBA, C-level officer ask me how to get something trademarked. So from my perspective, there's a great amount of confusion and apprehension when it comes to tackling branding and marketing issues in businesses across the board.

While branding is at its heart a "creative process," for many professionals it often sounds too soft and nebulous to have any tangible value. Nothing could be further from the truth. In this book, I'll walk you through a proven process that will show you how to find your niche, position the business, and develop a Bold Brand.

So what are you waiting for? Let's go!

Homework:

☐ How would you describe your brand today?

☐ Do you feel your firm has been a cutting-edge marketer, or just playing it safe?

☐ What branding questions have you asked?

☐ What branding and marketing opportunities are most obvious for your firm today?

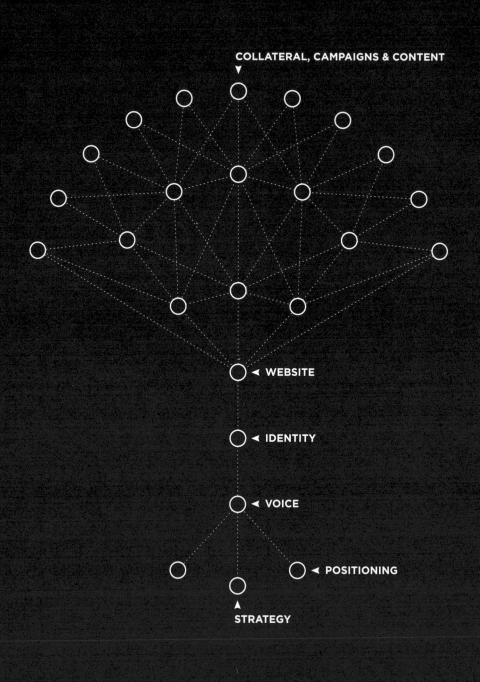

CHAPTER TWO

The Roots of Brand Strategy

Why you need a brand strategy for your business and where you should start.

> "For a tree to
> become tall it must
> grow tough roots
> among the rocks."
>
> —Friedrich Nietzsche

Regardless of an organization's size, developing strong roots in strategy is the single most important starting point for any branding exercise. And without a doubt, it's the most common step in the process to be met with resistance. There's an amazing amount of pushback when it comes to carving out a strategy on the front-end.

Why is that?

I think there are two prevalent problems in the marketing industry today that create this strategy-phobia.

The first problem with brand strategy:

Strategy sounds difficult and unattainable.

Strategy can sound awfully self-important; however, it's simply a word that means "plan of action." But before you can fully develop a plan of action, you need to know a few things about where you're starting from and where you want to go. Your brand strategy is that plan. Think of your brand strategy as the bottom layer of the brand pyramid, the roots from which everything else grows.

The second problem with brand strategy:

Creative firms allow clients to skip out on brand strategy.

Doesn't this seem counterintuitive? Why would a creative firm, supposedly "focused on your strategy to help build your brand," allow a client to skimp on strategy?

The reality is that most creative firms are more interested in creating the pretty, shiny deliverables (the graphic elements) and are happy to crank out another design. Later, they'll blame the client for "not getting it," and say, "what a shame they don't value our process."

How many times have you worked on a design exercise where the only deliverable was a "logo"? In the medical world, when physicians operate on their patients prior to performing a thorough diagnostic, it's called malpractice. Selling a "logo" without any strategy to back it up is just as bad; in fact, I call it marketing malpractice. This type of negligence creates a bad name for designers, marketers, and branding firms everywhere. It causes well-intentioned clients to form opinions that "branding is a waste of money," or worse yet, "branding doesn't work."

What can we learn about branding from trees?

One of the simplest ways to look at a brand is to think of it in the context of a tree. Trees and brands have much in common.

A tree inherently understands its role in the world. From its beginning as a seed, the DNA of the tree tells it exactly what it was designed to do, where it needs to grow, and how to thrive in its environment. When the seed comes to rest in the right spot, it begins to take root. It digs deep with an ever-expanding root system and reaches out to the sky with green, growing branches. As the young sapling feeds, it becomes the center of its own ecosystem.

Specific types of trees are easy to identify. They offer cues about what family they are from, what their use may be, and what kinds of animals might interact with them.

Different kinds of trees exist in distinct environments. They weather seasons of cold, rain, and extreme conditions. But no matter how mighty the tree, if even the tiniest invader is allowed to attack, it can spell the end for the tree.

Mighty trees also occasionally need maintenance. Whether it's nature's pruning through a windstorm, the occasional snack of an animal, or even the master gardener's discerning touch, trees may be cultivated to grow perfectly for their intended site, or twist and turn into a distorted existence. Pruning alone is not enough to encourage a tree to thrive in a location that isn't ideal for that tree.

Landscape designers must take into account the dimensions of width, breadth, height, and time. A small tree may fit perfectly into a space today, but in 30 years, will that location still best serve the tree and its surroundings?

Even novice gardeners understand the basics. When you plant a hardy tree in fertile ground and allow for plenty of sunshine and water, the result will be a healthy tree with a long, bright future. Other times it's not that simple. You may know that you want to grow a tree, but you understand that your environment is challenging. You may need a landscaping expert to provide guidance in order for your tree to thrive.

What about a gnarled tree that's aging and in bad shape? Well, unfortunately for the tree, it cannot decide one day to pursue a new strategy to become a majestic redwood.

A brand, on the other hand (with a lot of work and focus on the right things, in the right order), can overcome where it has been in the past.

Taking the time to consider each element of your brand will help to shape it into what you know it can be: a brand that will be easily recognized and well known. A brand that can be the center of its own ecosystem. A brand that can grow, adapt, and thrive with the seasons. And a brand that is easily differentiated from the rest of the brands in the forest.

Strategy requires a holistic, intentional approach.

A holistic branding exercise—the kind of exercise we're advocating here—requires every party involved (leadership, staff, consultants, and agency) to commit to a thorough diagnostic process.

The diagnosis can come in many forms. Often it's initiated by some sort of discovery meeting. Sometimes this process includes a series of interviews with the organization's leadership, management, internal stakeholders, clients, vendors, and even past clients. Other times it's a series of exercises with the internal marketing team, envisioning the future state of the organization, and finding which initiatives are the most advanced and which are the hollowest.

But in any case, the diagnosis almost always includes some type of audit or snapshot of anything and everything the organization touches: whether it's the company website, signage, on-hold messaging, sales presentations, or tradeshow materials. In some ways, it's a type of SWOT test, pointing out the strengths, weaknesses, opportunities, and threats to the brand as a whole.

Performing a brand audit.

A brand audit is the next step. For a new firm this probably isn't necessary, as there won't be much to audit. However, if you've been in business for several years, you may be surprised at the clues your past marketing efforts can provide for carving out your future Bold Brand.

Who should perform the brand audit? Every professional services firm is different, so there is no one-size-fits-all approach. Regardless of whether you assemble an in-house team or hire an outside consultant or agency, you need one very important thing: an honest objectivity.

An extensive brand audit should look at most of these categories:

Internal:

- Positioning
- Brand values
- Unique selling proposition (USP), brand promise, or brand essence
- Voice
- Culture
- Product/service positioning

External:

- Corporate identity—logos and other brand elements
- Collateral—brochures, print materials, tradeshow displays, etc.
- Advertising
- Website
- SEO
- Social media
- Sponsorships/civic involvement/memberships
- News/PR
- Content marketing and other assets—blogs, white papers, case studies, articles, books, etc.
- Testimonials
- Videos

Systems:

- Corporate identity/brand standards
- HR policies/on-boarding process
- Sales process/touch points
- Internal systems
- Customer service systems

ROI
Gut Check.

Brand Audit: Before and After.

In today's increasingly complex market, there is a hyper-focus (and rightfully so) on return on investment (ROI). Of course, ROI isn't just a tactic to keep the bean counters satisfied—weighing the financial benefits of your branding decisions throughout the process will help guide difficult decisions.

One way you can demonstrate ROI is by conducting a brand audit before and after a rebrand. This will show where the branding exercise helped improve systems and close gaps.

Do the math.

How many new clients/projects would you have to win to justify the costs of a rebrand?

For many professional services firms, one or two new clients would be more than enough to justify the investment.

Want to begin a brand audit on your own? See the section titled *DIY Bold Brand Audit* at the back of this book.

Homework:

☐ Picture your brand as a car. What kind would it be, and why? Would other people at your firm have different answers?

☐ Describe your brand as an animal, a tree, or even a movie star or pro athlete. This will help you think more abstractly about your brand.

☐ What type of ROI do you think you will achieve on your rebrand?

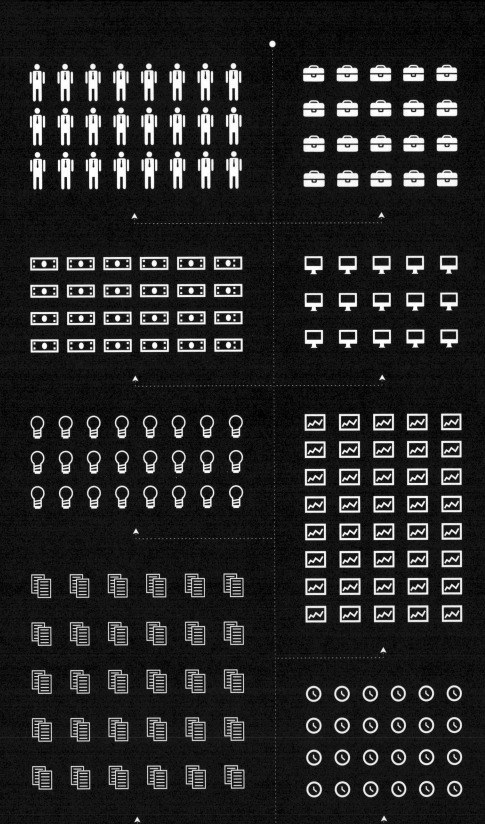

CHAPTER THREE

Business Goals & Objectives: Pick a Direction and Grow

Asking the tough questions to determine where to take your business and why.

"If you do not change direction, you may end up where you are heading."

—Lao Tzu

On the dark and crowded forest floor, the young sapling has one goal: grow toward the daylight. If the young tree grows in the wrong direction or fails to reach the daylight, its competition will grow faster and quickly block out the sunlight, greatly reducing its chances of survival.

Brand strategy isn't so different. It begins with asking tough questions, setting goals, and choosing where to go. Competition can be fierce, but worse yet is not knowing which direction to grow. Brand strategy is all about making future growth decisions. Before you decide which Pantone shade of orange your logo is going to be, or which keyword terms you want to dominate in Google searches, you need to make some intentional business decisions.

In the book *REWORK* by 37signals, co-authors Jason Fried, Heinemeier David Hansson, and Matthew Linderman say that "planning is guessing." They're absolutely right. Goals you set today may be far too short-sighted, and may even be laughable in 18 months. I'm certainly not advocating a 200-page financial projection to begin your branding process, but it's tough to arrive if you never decide where you want to go.

Our firm uses a prescriptive brand strategy process when working with clients. It always begins with asking questions such as:

- What are your business goals and objectives?

- What are you willing to invest to achieve your goals and objectives?

- Define your market, audience, and competition.

Perhaps your company hasn't thought through these questions. That's okay, but now is the time to wrap your head around them. The branding process by nature is very iterative. Future decisions are heavily influenced by the decisions you'll make today. Does that mean you can't change your mind in the future? Absolutely not. Adjusting business objectives or tweaking your priorities in the future is a natural part of doing business.

What are your business goals and objectives?

That's a loaded question. Thinking about your business goals is a big picture question. Big picture questions can be overwhelming to think through because sometimes they're so vague that it's difficult to consider them, or so general that any answer would be somewhat correct.

Technically, this isn't one question. There are other questions behind this question. So instead of viewing "what are your business goals and objectives?" as the question itself, think of it as the big bucket that carries lots of smaller buckets. Smaller buckets are the smaller questions and are easier to focus on. For many of our clients, here's where we start:

- **What were your sales over the last three years?** What are your sales goals for this year, next year, and five years out? Are there any products or services in particular that you'd like to sell more of? Are there any products or services that have become less profitable, that you'd like to phase out?

- **What are your personnel goals for this year?** If you hit your sales goal, how will that impact your staffing needs? Is your senior leadership team missing any vital positions? Do you need more administrative help, more producers, or more business development support?

- **What are your client goals?** Do you need to bring in one new client this year, or 100? Do you need to increase your book of business, or change the types of clients you engage with? Or would you be better off servicing fewer clients at a deeper, more profitable level?

- **What are your thought leadership goals?** Are you viewed as an expert in your field? Does the media come to you—or your competition—for insight when something happens in your industry? Do you have a "following" online?

- **Do you have a sales process goal?** Do you need to generate more leads to add to your sales funnel, or do you need to refine your current database?

- **Do you have a positioning or perception goal?** Do your current clients understand all that you do and the level at which you perform? Do your current clients use a competitor for services that you currently offer? Does the marketplace understand the unique value that you provide?

- **Where do your leads come from?** Are there particular lead-generation tools that should be more productive for you, like speaking engagements or your website?

- **What are your business objectives for your website this year?** Do you want to improve your search engine optimization (SEO)? What keywords do you want to dominate? How many leads should your website generate? Do you need to improve your conversion rate? How many subscribers should your blog have? What are your social media goals?

What are you willing to invest to achieve your goals and objectives?

When you build a great brand, you invest more than money. You invest time, energy, and focus.

But first, let's talk cash.

There's an old saying in the marketing profession that I suspect gets used in other circles as well: "You can have it fast, good, or cheap. Pick two."

This definitely applies to building a great brand. If you want a great brand you probably can do all the work yourself and spend more time on it, or you can get professional help and invest more money in the process to have it done faster.

What should a branding process cost? A conservative marketing budget should be somewhere between 1 to 4% of your annual gross sales. If you're an aggressive start-up or in a more competitive market space, you might consider upwards of 10 to 15% of gross sales. A strong, differentiated brand is far more cost-effective to market than an unprofessional, me-too product or service. Branding should be viewed either as a capital investment or part of your marketing budget. Regardless of where you decide to account for the expense, you need to consider your total marketing budget as a good place to begin.

Time.

Who's going to be responsible for creating your new brand? Will you hire a branding firm, or try to do this in-house? It's more than a question of budget; it's also a question of how much time you'll need to invest personally to see this come to fruition.

A branding firm should involve you with vital decisions during the process, and keep you updated in more minor areas. Ideally, the branding process should not be a total time-suck for you and your team. However, the more you leave on your own shoulders, the more you should expect to burn the midnight oil to get things right. You also need to consider the opportunity cost of doing it yourself. If you're working on your own branding, you're not doing billable client work.

Another element of the "time investment" is your timeline. Is there a particular upcoming event that you'd like to have your new brand ready for? Is there a particular time of year that generates the most sales? We see many clients who, once they've committed to a branding exercise, want everything done yesterday. Realistically though, developing a great brand takes time. Depending on the depth of the exercise and size of your organization, expect to invest anywhere from several months to a year to properly position, roll out, and market your new brand.

Energy and focus.

When a professional services firm is preparing to engage in a rebranding effort, one question I am usually asked is, "How much time are you going to need from me and my staff to make sure this is successful?"

I'm not sure if there's a right or wrong answer here. I think most professionals like to feel as if they're quarterbacking anything they are hired to do. And when it comes to professionals working for other professionals, this is where some territorial issues can occur. Everyone is used to being in control. Therefore, it's a good idea to discuss expectations from the outset. The bottom line is, it's important to understand the process and communication style of your branding partner. You'll want to have a good idea of how much input they'll need from you and your team, as well as how much ongoing legwork they'll expect from you.

Going back to our good, fast, or cheap example, if you selected cheap, there's a good chance you're going to have more work to do on your side of the fence.

Define your market, audience, and competition.

Once you've made it through the big questions of business goals, objectives, timeline, and budget, these next few questions will seem like a cinch.

What is your market category?

Your market category should be a simple statement that

identifies your brand's general sphere of competition.

For our clients, we want to make sure their market category is crystal clear and as tightly defined as possible. It's natural to think that we're pigeonholing them by doing this, but if we don't get explicit in stating their core area of business, it will cause problems differentiating them later in the process.

For instance, instead of saying your market is "engineering," we might say "interstate highway and bridge design and civil engineering." Or instead of saying "catering," we might say "premium catering for special events."

Of course, you know what your company does, but when you describe it to others, do they really get it? Once you get it down on paper, your market category may surprise you a little. Or, it may confirm what you already suspected was true.

Who is your audience?

Who buys your product or service? Who should be buying from you? Where are they? Do you service a specific geographic area, region, or country? Can people buy from you online or internationally? What do your customer profiles look like?

Again, we try to be specific with the answers to these questions, but there is often more than one audience type. The audience may look something like this:

Professional services firms, funded start-ups, or Software as a Service (SaaS) companies:

- Chief marketing officer, vice president of marketing or communications

- CEO, partner, or vice president of operations

Small venture capital or private equity firms:

- Managing member or partner responsible for marketing of portfolio companies

Business coaches:

- Executive coaches who make marketing recommendations for clients.

Who is your competition?

If you're lucky, this is a short list. But most companies have competitors at various levels. If your firm is multidisciplinary like ours, you may face different competitors based on which service you're thinking of. An offset printing company has to compete at some level both with the shop down the street, and the likes of instyprints.com. Your competition isn't always your peers. Sometimes it's less apples-to-apples, and more like an apple, an orange, and a banana.

As you list your competitors, think about them along the lines of product, service, price, quality, reputation, and location. Make a list of all competitors in each category. From that list, create a visual to show where your real competition is, and where your positioning opportunities lie. It's called perceptual mapping. Specifically, this is your perception of your competition.

Once you have your lists done, select two categories that make the most sense to compare. For example, you might compare quality versus price.

Next, create a simple chart with a horizontal and vertical axis. Along the horizontal axis, map the elements of your competition's quality. At the left end will be lower-end competitors, and to the right will live more customized competitors. Now along the vertical axis compare pricing—

the cheapest offerings live at the bottom and the higher you go along the vertical axis, the more expensive the offerings. Place marks not only where your product or service goes, but also where your direct and indirect competitors' products and services land. After you plot this first chart, get creative. Compare other things like geographic market or size of company.

Where does your company fall on the map?

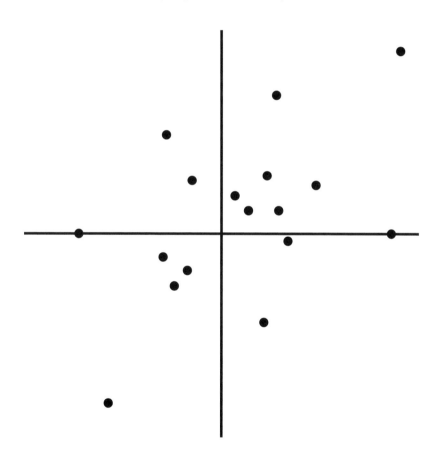

FIGURE A: **COMMODITY**

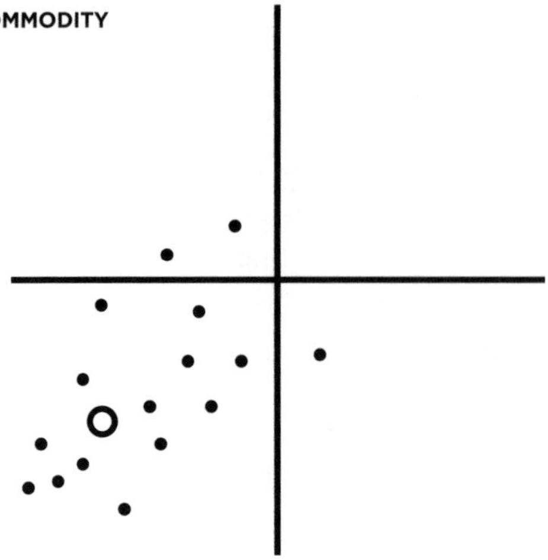

FIGURE B: **PREMIUM**

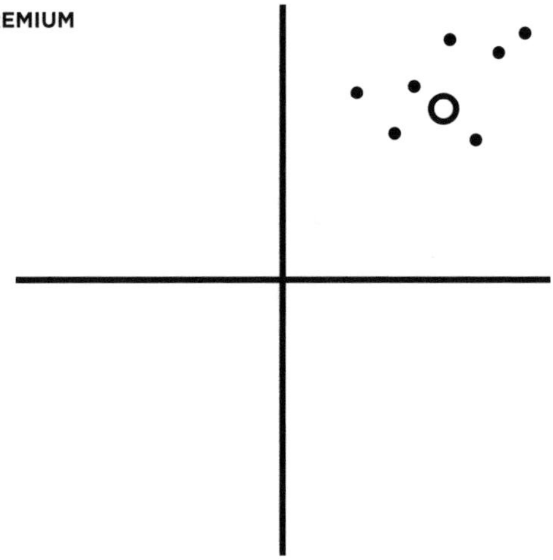

FIGURE C: **CROWDED**

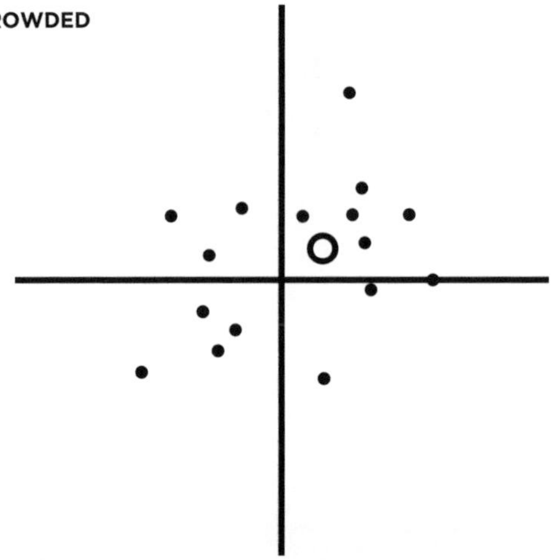

If your chart looks like Figure A (low and to the left with lots of surrounding dots), you're probably in a commodity business. Your positioning opportunities are a) command a higher price through value, brand, or service, or b) get more market share.

If you're in the commodity space, focus on finding an intangible way to differentiate your product or service. In the 1940s, advertising legend Rosser Reeves called this "thing" your unique selling proposition (USP). Paper towels are just paper towels, right? Not if they're the "quicker picker upper."

If your chart looks like Figure B (high and to the right, with a few surrounding dots), you're likely a premium product or service. In the premium world, your positioning—by definition—is already pretty set. You're distinguished, and as such, you charge more. Positioning is less of a tool to explore, and more of a status to maintain. Strong, consistent branding is the best way to maintain your premium status.

Conversely, if your chart looks like most businesses (Figure C), you have several positioning opportunities. The middle of your chart is a crowded place, but the corners are opportunities. What could you remove from your offering to make it dirt cheap and dominate the marketplace? What could you add to your service to charge three times more? Or how could you operate in the midst of the competition and still stand out? Perhaps you could leverage your USP or differentiate yourself through design or reputation.

Homework:

☐ What goals and objectives are most
important for your firm right now?

☐ What do you need to do as a firm to
accomplish those goals and objectives?

☐ Who is your audience?

☐ Who is your competition?

☐ What role will budget play in accomplishing
your most important objectives?

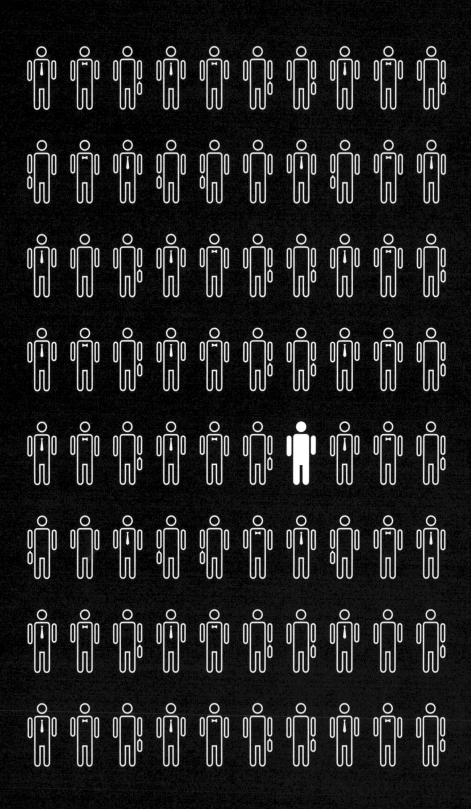

CHAPTER FOUR

Positioning & Differentiation

One of the biggest challenges for any business is figuring out how to be different. How do you stand out as a unique offering in the marketplace?

> "Who are you? Who, who, who, who?"
>
> —Pete Townshend, The Who

How do you look different and sound different from your competition? It's so tempting to jump straight into a purely visual exercise...but first you have to answer the question, "Who are you?"

I'm thinking of a frog.

"I'm thinking...of a frog."

Mr. Waldron had a way of delivering new concepts unlike any teacher I've ever known. He sat motionless in his chair in the back corner of the room. My AP Literature classmates and I were familiar with his behavior at this point, but today was somehow different. The lights were down low. Nobody knew if they were supposed to respond, or just continue to sit quietly. He started in again: "I'm thinking...of a frog."

"Kermit?" someone mused.

"I'm sorry, but that's not the frog I was thinking of."

"The little ones with the big red eyes? Is that the frog?"

"I'm sorry, but that's not the frog I was thinking of."

"It's when I can't seem to speak right? There's a frog in my throat?"

Again he only offered, "I'm sorry, but that's not the frog I was thinking of."

Crap. What was it going to take for someone to figure this out?

Waldron taunted us again. "I'm thinking...of a frog."

One of the students, a first-chair violinist, offered, "It's on my violin bow. It's the piece at the end that I hold onto."

"Yes, that is a frog," Waldron said with a little more pep. "But... that's not the frog I was thinking of."

If you can imagine, this went on for the entire 90-minute period. And at the end of class he simply said, "Have a nice day." No explanation. No debriefing. Just "have a nice day."

That single class messed me up. I think it left a lasting impression on all of us.

During our next class with Waldron, he explained that he wasn't thinking of any frog in particular. The point was to demonstrate how clearly we need to communicate. Even with such a specific noun as "frog," the recipient of your message can be left very unsure of what you are trying to say. As I would later learn in a college communications class, message sent does not equal message received.

Today I can't help but think of the parallels. Clarity and messaging. Positioning and marketing. Top-of-mind awareness, and this thing we call brand.

People are thinking about "frogs"—products, services, or solutions to their needs, wants, or incredibly difficult problems— all the time. They know exactly which frog they're thinking of, and there are several reasons why. Will your brand be the frog they think of first?

Perhaps your customer is thinking of a frog.

What do you stand for? What do you believe? Who are you, really? Are you different enough to be memorable? Positioning is the art and science of getting to the bottom of some of these questions.

Do you have a positioning problem? Many businesses don't think so, at least not at first.

Have you ever had a client share with you, "I didn't know you guys did that?" Have you ever found out after the fact that many of your competitors were bidding on a project that you were unaware of? Can all of your staff quickly rattle off an elevator pitch for who you are and what you do—something that won't make you cringe? Does your receptionist know what your firm specializes in? If your dream client walked into your office while you were on vacation, would your team know what to do with that person—or even recognize him or her as a great prospect?

If any of these questions concern you, there's a good chance you have a positioning problem. Don't worry...most businesses have a positioning problem at some level. Businesses evolve, the market's needs change, and new technologies are constantly in flux. Positioning is constantly in need of attention...which is not an excuse to ignore it.

There are many different elements to positioning. Some of these include:

Where are you located? How close are you to your client base? Do you have a "bricks and mortar" presence or is your business virtual?

Who is your client or customer? Do you target specific demographic or psychographic profiles? Do you target certain industries or a specific size of business?

What do you do? Do you sell a product or a service? Is it a unique product or can your competitors sell it as well? Is your service performed by skilled laborers, thinkers, or hourly employees? Accenture and Walmart may both believe they are in the service business, but both companies have very different goals, clients, and employees. What you "do" is the tip of the positioning iceberg. When you're in the professional services business, others can see this tip. However, there are many more things you do that are all but invisible to most clients, acquaintances, and prospects.

Have you ever considered your mission or vision? What are they? You need a real mission statement, not a motivational poster statement.

When I ask this question it's usually a trap. I hate most mission statements with a passion. I don't hate them because they're inherently a bad idea. I hate them because (in my very scientific estimation) 99 percent of them are generic, bland, and forgettable.

A few years ago I was asked to present to a professional group about website design. I was asked to discuss corporate website basics—what websites need and where most go astray.

If I remember correctly, the first words out of my mouth were, "Take your mission statement off of your homepage, because nobody cares." I think I had their attention.

Do you see anything unique about the "mission" of the companies who wrote the following statements:

> "Our team members are the foundation of our company's commitment to excellence. We pledge to provide team members with appreciation, recognition, and a nurturing environment. Our team members will learn, grow, and have confidence and courage to provide exceptional service."

> "Our continuing goal is to achieve excellence by providing every client with the highest quality of service."

> "At XYZ Corp, our goal is to provide for your needs in the best possible manner."

It's not that these mission statements aren't nice sounding. It's that they are trite, undifferentiated, and uninspired. Who doesn't want to provide every client with the highest quality of service? Who shouldn't strive to meet their client's needs in the best possible manner? Who doesn't want a confident and exceptional team? Unfortunately, when it comes to mission statements, it's not the thought that counts.

I'm giving you two choices here: lose the mission statement altogether or do it right.

The bottom line is that a weak mission statement often reflects poor positioning. Which should come first, the mission or the positioning? I'll be the first to admit it can seem like a bit of a chicken/egg question. But we always prefer to begin by developing strong positioning and then let the mission statement flow from that language. We'll dive deeper into positioning in the next chapter.

What if your company already has a mission statement and you can't decide if it's a good starting point for your positioning? Let's talk about this a little more.

If you're going to have a mission statement at all, it should be the guiding light that directs the course of your business. Let's look at four approaches to writing a mission statement that people will understand.

First, focus on the facts.

What do you do? What is your product or service? What is your market? How far is your reach? What words does your company use to describe its services? This step should be pretty straightforward. Once you've wrapped up, move on to step two.

Second, think about the emotions.

How does your organization make the world a better place? Who does your company benefit? Who would miss you if your organization disappeared? Why should anyone care? Make a list of some of the most emotionally charged benefits of your company. Once you've given this ample consideration, move on to step three. Still scratching your head? If you're stuck on this one, consider enlisting help from someone who knows your company well, but has an outsider's or more objective point of view.

Third, focus on the unique.

What is the one thing that you do better than anyone else? Are you the best at it in your market or region? Can you claim "only-ness?" Complete this sentence: We are the only (blank) in (blank) that does (blank). When you fill in the blanks what do you get? If it sounds the same as your competition, you may need to dig deeper. Give this plenty of thought before moving on to step four.

And lastly, simplify, simplify, simplify.

Taking what may be several pages of notes from the exercises above, begin simplifying the message into statements. If you're really focused, you may be able to distill it down to a few succinct words. One of our executive coaching clients has its corporate mission statement polished down to two words. "Inspire Hope."

A two-word mission statement isn't right for everyone, but if your mission is unclear, ambiguous or wordy, keep working.

A few more words of advice: the senior leaders of your company need to own the mission statement. Hiring a professional writer may be a good move, but limit who gets a vote on the final mission statement.

That's important. No mission statement committees!

Are you communicating your positioning with the megaphone or the wedge?

Most new business owners are so excited about their company's capabilities that they will bowl over their friends and family when trying to explain the breadth of their company's offerings. "We do this, and this, and that, and even this other thing, but our specialty is blah. Except last week, this one company asked us to do this totally different thing, so we thought we could probably figure it out. They've really got us hopping. And then they asked us to help them get their email and computers hooked up to the Internet. We don't know anything about that stuff, but we eventually figured it out! Does your company need any of that?"

You always feel sorry for the poor soul who gets cornered by this guy at a cocktail party or networking event. Even if you were trying to pay attention to the story, you'd likely walk away thinking this guy was a "jack of all trades and master of none." The chances you'd hire him for his specialty or even remember what his specialty was after all of that are about nil.

The problem was he hit you with the broad side of his capabilities iceberg. It's deep, blunt, cold, and too much for anyone to take. Even the Titanic couldn't handle the impact of the broadside of an iceberg.

Blair Enns, founder of Win Without Pitching, is a business consultant to marketing and creative firms. He calls this "the wedge." If you lead with the blunt side of the wedge, there's impact for sure, but it's too broad of an angle to ever pierce your audience's armor. To do it right, you have to turn the wedge around, and attack with the pointy part—the armor-piercing side of the wedge.

Let's go back to our cocktail party example above. Instead of listening to our friend, let's say you're the one who is asked, "So what do you do?" Being a fantastic networker, you respond with something like, "We help take the stress out of day-to-day bookkeeping for small business owners." One of several things is likely to happen next.

1. Immediate need. Your friend might immediately think of how this could help him or someone he knows. With one little tease, you have opened the door for him to learn more about your business. His earnest interest in learning more may sound like, "That's one of our biggest pains. How can you guys help a mid-sized firm like ours?"

2. Plant the seed. Although he may not have an immediate need, don't lose heart. Your words probably resonated with him on some level. "We just hired a new temp to help with bookkeeping, but I'll keep you guys in mind if this doesn't work out as we planned."

3. A future lead. Maybe your friend will be able to quickly determine your service is not a fit for his firm. And that's okay. Sometimes there's a zero percent chance you and your new friend will ever be able to do business together but regardless, your "sticky" message still stay with him. The next time he is asked for a bookkeeping referral, he might remember this conversation. This sounds more like, "Oh, my father's company handles that for us. They're always looking for contractors though—do you know of any good ones looking for work?"

Regardless of how real the opportunity is once you've "pierced the armor," as Blair Enns says, the point is you've pierced it. You've positioned your company for something very specific, and are much more likely to be remembered by your new friend. Good work. But how do you get to that armor-piercing positioning statement?

The trick is to get to a narrower positioning than many

businesses are comfortable with. Or as we say in the marketing world, your goal should be to find your niche.

Chances are you aren't operating from a niche position today. Let's say your firm is in the information technology business. An IT business is a fun one to pick on. First of all, hardly anyone (except for other IT professionals) knows what the heck IT is, and what it's not. What does your IT business do?

Can you run wire? Can you set up a network? Can you get my phone to connect to Gmail? Can you format my flash drive? Will you install Windows on our spare laptop? Can you figure out why important emails are getting caught in our spam filter? Do you work on Macs or PCs? Why won't my iPod sync with my office machine? Can you help me set up FTP? Will you make updates to our website? Can you create a backup and disaster recovery plan for our file server? And what about the cloud? Does your firm offer virtualized services or backup data in the cloud? (The concept of cloud computing is confusing enough for most people, but the way so many firms toss it around on their websites, it's no wonder your clients don't understand.)

The funny thing is, for most IT companies, the answer to all of the above questions may be "yes," but most of them should be saying "no" if they ever want to create a more profitable position for themselves in the minds of their clients.

What if instead of saying "yes" to all of these questions, your IT firm were to specialize in Apple products, limiting the list above substantially? Would that mean you couldn't help with other small jobs as needed? Of course not, but your customer base would be reduced to one operating system, greatly reducing the amount of education and experience your employees would require.

To think of niche positioning another way, does your company today have any competition?

Take a moment to think about who your "competition" really is. You probably immediately thought of one or two competitors. Your prospects may even ask you about them. Your competitors are busy pitching for the same accounts that you're pursuing.

What if you could make them go away? I don't mean out of business or even out of town. But what would it take to prevent them from being able to compete with your company altogether? The reality is, you can't actually get them to "go anywhere," but there is a very simple solution.

Make your competition invisible by getting out of their business. Niche yourself so far away, that you'll never see your competition again.

It's all about positioning. If you're familiar with the concept of Blue Ocean Strategy, finding an untapped, wide-open market is awesome. The truth is you may not have to be quite that radical. The truth is, if you take a page out of the Seth Godin playbook and just do something remarkable, you're halfway there.

A great first step is to define a niche. "But I don't want to pigeonhole our company with a niche!" Yep, think of all of those poor, under-performing niche brands: North Face (just for hikers), Geek Squad (just for home computer repairs), and Apple computers (just for creative types).

Niche positioning doesn't limit your market—it expands it.

Why is that? When a consumer thinks, "I really need an XYZ," whatever brand fulfills that niche positioning will be the first brand the consumer will think of.

So how do we apply what we see in the consumer product market to the professional services market?

First, let's remember that the same "30-year-old dude" who's buying North Face and Apple could be the same professional who's making the decision about which architects to consider for the building expansion, or which law firm would be best suited to handle intellectual property matters. People are people. When they're at work, they're still people. You aren't selling to a "business." More than likely, you're selling to another person. Don't forget that.

Five easy methods to identify your niche.

So back to the question, how can we go about applying what we know in the consumer market to the professional services market? Here are my top five suggestions:

1. Find a price niche.

What would your customers be willing to pay a premium for? Within your market, what can you offer at the top end of the price spectrum? Or how can you bill differently? If your industry typically bills by the hour, consider offering a fixed bid for project work, or even a flat monthly retainer. On the flip side, what can you systematize and charge a miniscule amount for? What if you became known as the giant law firm that files trademark applications as fast as the online guys, but with the clout and service that you're known for in the community?

2. Look for low-hanging fruit.

What do your customers want that you (and your competitors) don't currently offer? How can you take your service to the next level? Daily personal telephone updates? On-site service? Online project status monitoring? A project manager with an iPhone could easily post progress photos of your new building and status updates via Twitter. (Hint: This may be the thing from #1 that allows you to charge a premium.)

At our office, the dry cleaner picks up our laundry from our suite and delivers it right back to our coat closet. My credit card is on file, and I seldom even see our trusty delivery guy. It's like magic. And guess what? It costs pretty much the same as the strip-mall dry cleaner. Remarkable.

3. Before you try to look different, figure out how to be different.

Design and marketing professionals are experts in the art of creating something new and interesting. This works out great when you ARE new and interesting. However, if you're really more of the same old, same old, it tends to backfire. Arguably one of the best "brands" in history for doing something different: Barack Obama. He sounded different, he exploited his differences, and he did an amazing job of looking different. Now we get to see if he lives up to his brand promise of Hope and Change.

4. If you're doing something different, be sure you look and sound different.

Imagine this: You have designed a game-changing, professional services offering. And now that it's time to take it to market, you decide to mimic your closest competitor's brand identity, design, brand voice, and advertisements. Given all of these similar visuals and messages, why on earth would anyone expect your service to actually be different, let alone better? If your aim is to truly be remarkable, take it all the way. Imitation in the world of branding is the sincerest form of shooting yourself in the foot.

5. Ask a trusted advisor.

Chances are you're so close to your own brand that you're still a bit confused. You may have even convinced yourself that you're well-niched and highly differentiated. Strangely enough, your competition is still there, buzzing in your ear. Now would be a good time to get a second opinion. Ask a mentor, a colleague in a different profession, or even an outside marketing professional.

Here's one final suggestion: When you're looking for an outside firm to help with your positioning, branding, or marketing, ask them why they are unique. And then ask them who their competition is. If their answers sound similar to yours, keep looking.

Homework:

☐ Define your firm's true points of differentiation.

☐ Do you have a strong mission or vision statement—or a motivational poster statement?

☐ Is your firm communicating your positioning with a megaphone or a wedge?

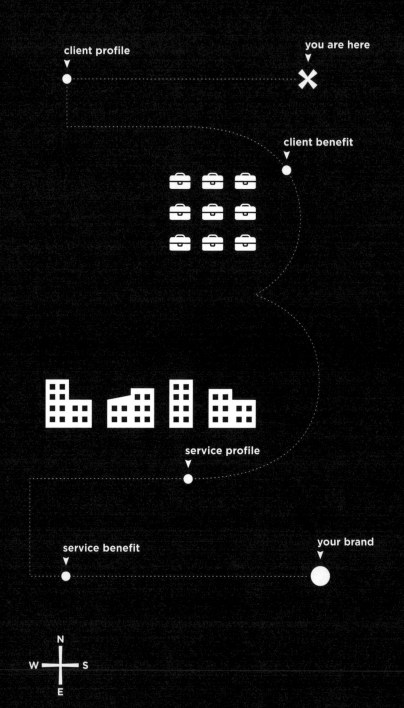

CHAPTER FIVE

The Positioning Brief: Finding Your Brand Essence

How to keep everyone in your organization on the same page.

> "Be a yardstick of quality. Some people aren't used to an environment where excellence is expected."
>
> —Steve Jobs

What is your brand essence?

Branding and positioning exercises can be great team-building experiences for your senior leadership. It's exciting to embark on a rebranding process and it can be energizing for everyone involved. But it will all be a waste of time if you don't make everyone within the organization aware of your new direction.

To keep everyone on the same page, you need some type of document that will serve as a guidepost. When our firm works with a client on a branding initiative, we create a document that we call the Bold Brand™ positioning brief. In this chapter, I'll walk you through how you can follow the same process with your brand.

The positioning brief is an internal document developed to ensure that everything your organization says, does, or plans—from branding, to advertising, to annual sales meetings to lapel pins—consistently leverages the factors that set you apart.

Your Bold Brand positioning brief should be organized into the following short sections:

- Our market category

- Who we are

- Who we aren't

- What we believe

- Our brand essence.

Let's take a look at each.

Our market category.

The goal here is to explicitly state your market category. This is a simple statement, usually four words or less. Don't elaborate on the firm's business plan or delve into the principal's experience. Simply identify the brand's general sphere of competition. For example:

> *Architects of public spaces*

Your brand category probably won't surprise you very much; instead, it will probably confirm what you already suspected was true, in a very concise statement.

Who we are.

This section begins to specifically address the factors that make you unique. It references the physical, intellectual, or attitudinal aspects of your product or organization. In a single paragraph, it should touch upon the most striking attributes of your product or service:

> *We design iconographic spaces that become the visual language of a community, and the soundtrack of its life experience. We focus on sustainable approaches to new construction and historic preservation alike. Our buildings become the standard for how public spaces should feel.*

Who we aren't.

Pointing out who you are not can help your team get a clearer picture of exactly who you are. To that end, your positioning statement should provide information that helps you define your niche:

We aren't strip mall designers, or architects who find the cheapest way to create a project. We aren't disconnected from the community, or merely involved in hopes of winning another award. And most importantly, we won't use a material that will compromise the aesthetics, integrity, or our planet in the process when a superior option is available.

What we believe.

At this point, we're less interested in mere description. This paragraph serves as a manifesto that helps the attitude of your brand take shape. It reflects the values and emotional aspects of your brand. And that's important. Decisions are almost always based on emotion:

We believe our work is deeper than designing a building or a space. We believe we are designing the experiences of this generation and generations to come. We believe that your mood, attitude, and state of mind will be impacted just by being surrounded by our work. We believe iconographic architecture defines the very heart of a place.

Service Profile:
A short list of the most striking characteristics of your service.

Client Profile:
Qualities that outline the general profile of your target audience.

Bold Brand Essence:
This is the sweet spot where the unique elements of your brand intersect. It will be a precise statement pinpointing the core of your Bold Brand. It is the shortest, cleanest description of who you are.

Client Benefit:
The key benefit (or benefits) derived from the product or service's profile.

Service Benefit:
What benefits are most likely to be felt by your prospective audience?

Our brand essence.

What comes next? At this point, you have several stakes in the ground and a clearer idea about how your organization intends to be viewed in the marketplace. You understand your competition, goals, values, and how you want to be seen. What you don't have yet is a single phrase from which you can articulate your position and your brand.

> *We believe this single idea...this single phrase...can be found at the point where the unique elements of your brand intersect.*

How can you visualize this? Picture a giant X. The left leg is your product/service leg, and the right leg is your consumer/audience leg. At the top of the X are your profiles, and at the bottom are the benefits.

Product/service profile.

Create a short list of the most striking characteristics of your product or services:

> *Museums, monuments, stadiums, and iconographic corporate headquarters design and architecture.*

Consumer/audience profile.

Think about the general profile of your target audience. Who are they and where are they found:

> *CEOs, trustees, board members, and leaders of visionary and progressive American cities, schools, and enterprises.*

Product/service benefits.

Explain the key benefit (or benefits) derived from the product or service. Consider what really differentiates your firm:

> *Buildings and spaces that become renowned as icons for a city, school, or place.*

Consumer/audience benefits.

What benefits are most likely to be felt by your prospective audience? (Any rules that we set in our previous chapter on mission statements apply here as well.) It may help to actually picture a person saying this statement:

> *"This building/monument/space has become synonymous with our city/school/company. People can't get enough of it and rave that the emotions they feel when they are here have forever enhanced their feelings toward us."*

At the intersection of these legs, you'll find your Bold Brand sweet spot. From here, you will be able to craft a precise statement that captures the core essence of your brand, i.e., your brand essence statement. It is the shortest, cleanest description of who you are.

When you see it all together, here's how the brand essence statement using our example would read:

> *Revealing the heart and soul of place.*

For many of our clients, the brand essence statement becomes an internal rallying cry, a tagline, or the building block for future voice and messaging exercises. A company's brand essence is a very personal thing. For this reason, we often consider several alternate brand essence statements. It's sort of like trying on a shoe—you'll know the one that fits best and feels most comfortable.

The brand essence chart is a powerful tool that helps firms "visualize" who they really are. In fact, one of our clients recently shared, "We've been trying to succinctly state 'who we are' for years. We finally have something that we can all point to and speak the same language. I love it!"

Service Profile:
Museums, monuments, stadiums, and iconographic corporate headquarters design and architecture.

Client Profile:
CEOs, trustees, board members, and leaders of visionary and progressive cities, schools, and enterprises.

Bold Brand Essence:

Revealing the heart and soul of place.

Client Benefit:
"This space has become synonymous with our organization, forever enhancing our visitors' feelings toward us."

Service Benefit:
Buildings and spaces that become renowned as icons for a city, school, or place.

Homework:

☐ How would you fill out your positioning brief?

☐ Which sections seem most challenging?

☐ How could visualizing your Bold Brand sweet spot help you with other strategic decisions?

Window Dressing

Fresh Face

Brand Overhaul

CHAPTER SIX

Three Approaches to Rebranding

There are three key reasons why organizations rebrand and one of them in particular "ain't good."

> "There are three things that can happen when you pass, and two of them ain't good."
>
> —Coach Woody Hayes

Branding
=
Problem Solving.

In football, a team's approach is driven by one goal: score more points than the opposition. Sure, there are probably other things the team hopes to accomplish along the way. Improve special teams. Make fewer errors. But ultimately, it's about winning.

Likewise, as varied as the contributing factors may be for rebranding, an organization's one goal can probably be boiled down to one thing as well: make more money.

Of course, there are a few different approaches a company might consider to achieve this goal, but before we dig into what these approaches look like, let's first explore the contributing factors that lead organizations to rebrand.

What drives an organization to rebrand in the first place?

Professional services firms and other businesses choose to rebrand for a variety of reasons. Sometimes it's a merger or acquisition of another company. Sometimes it's a shift in their approach or business model. Sometimes companies rebrand to shed excess baggage or negative PR. And sometimes it's just time to dust-off a dated look and refresh their position in the market.

When an organization is willing to invest time and effort into rebranding, they typically have a problem they are trying to solve or a milestone they hope to achieve. It may be an internal issue, such as poor morale, management, or lack of systems. It may be an external issue, such as an outdated appearance. It could be driven by a target to double sales or expand to a new market. Or it may be a combination of problems they seek to overcome and goals they hope to achieve.

Branding = problem solving

At its root, isn't that what good branding does? It helps organizations solve problems.

The problem-solving characteristics of branding are derived from its roots in business strategy and design.

Design is problem solving? Isn't design just another word for "decorating"? I can't fault anyone for thinking of design as the act of making something look better, prettier, cooler, or more cutting-edge. This very well could be what most people think the word design means.

However, take a minute to look up "design" in the dictionary. In most cases, you'll find a description of purpose, planning, intention, and thought behind something. It's important to see branding as an extension of this type of planning and intentional problem solving. A branding exercise that does not seek to solve a problem will yield a lackluster end product.

Branding isn't the only strategy that can help a company achieve goals or solve problems. A variety of business decisions could greatly impact a company's ability to reach new heights. A company could choose to invest in infrastructure, talent, seek investment, or even relocate to a new, high-profile location.

However, rebranding is an optimal strategy for any company to consider when seeking to solve an "awareness" problem. Companies that choose to rebrand are likely to see their awareness problem as a primary roadblock to accomplishing their number one goal: growing the bottom line.

Awareness takes many shapes.

Any company that has been in business for awhile surely has some awareness in the marketplace. If they didn't, they probably wouldn't still be in business. That much is clear.

However, is it the right kind of awareness? What is the market's impression of their company? Do targets understand the breadth of the company's capabilities? Let's look at the different shapes that awareness problems may take:

Unaware

Awareness is a funny thing. One organization may have an "awareness problem" because nobody knows they exist, or they have simply been flying under the radar. Of course, their current clients and vendors are aware of them. However, if their goal is to reach more clients and grow the bottom line, they need more awareness in the marketplace.

Consider the seemingly "new" footwear brand, UGG Australia. UGG boots have been sold in Australia since 1982, but only began enjoying name recognition in the U.S. market 10 years ago.

Or think about the "new" rock act, The Black Keys. Although their popularity has spiked since winning Grammy awards in 2010, this duo has been making music since 2001. While it's common for quality music to go unnoticed for a long time, if people don't know about your band, you have an awareness problem.

Unfavorable awareness

Another organization may think the world has a negative impression of them. Whether the negative reputation was rightfully earned (or not), it's an awareness problem that must be dealt with.

Recent mergers and maturing businesses are good examples of this awareness problem. Think of the "new" AT&T, which was a merger of SBC (formerly AT&T) and Cingular Wireless. Or Skype, which received some interesting comments across social media after announcing it would be acquired by Microsoft. As a small, cutting-edge company, Skype is now dealing with some potentially negative expectations of what a Microsoft Skype product may have to endure to continue to innovate.

Limited awareness

Awareness also comes into play when your business model shifts or you add a new capability. Is the market aware of exactly what you do now, and why it should matter to them?

Brands that recently overcame this type of awareness challenge include the emergence of McDonald's and Dunkin' Donuts in the "gourmet" coffee space. Both companies were best known previously for their food offerings, and yet both have launched impressive national campaigns for a space once dominated by Starbucks. Do you think of either of these two brands now when you want a good cup of coffee?

Likewise, Kia and Hyundai have each made an impressive push to be seen as legitimate choices in the American automobile market. Their fresh new product designs are evidence of an attempt to shift our awareness of their products and reposition these brands in the minds of U.S. consumers. Is it working for you?

What other brands can you think of that have tackled their awareness problems? How did they solve these problems?

Solving awareness problems.

Rebranding efforts most commonly fall under one of three approaches. We could explore other approaches, but in the end, those could probably be classified as a variation of one of the following:

1. Window dressing

"We have concerns with our reputation and our brand. Although many of our problems are directly related to our internal operations, organization, and customer service, we hope our new look will help improve our reputation in the marketplace."

2. A fresh face on a great place

"We have a great company, but a dated presence in the market. We want our brand to be seen as positively on the outside, as we see our organization internally."

3. Total brand overhaul, inside and out

"Our brand is in rough shape. We have internal problems and external problems in the marketplace. We know it's time to overhaul how we do things, and we're thinking through every possible touch point, both inside our organization and in the marketplace."

Let's take a look at each.

First approach: Window dressing.

It's not uncommon for organizations that are dealing with internal problems to think that "updating their look" may help improve public perception, and in the end, their bottom line. However, if this "window dressing" isn't accompanied by real change within, the rebranding effort at best will flop, and at worst, completely backfire.

So what's wrong with simply wanting your brand to "look better"?

Nothing—just be sure that the visual update is accompanied by real change in the company, product, or service.

Think about the Yugo automobile brand. Not only did the product leave much to be desired, but in the late 80s, the brand name itself was a common punch line on late night television. Clearly a visual update alone would not have provided a long-term boost for the company.

If you think a little "window dressing" can solve your brand's reputation issues long-term, you're fooling yourself. Anytime an organization rebrands but fails to live up to its new image, that's an approach that "ain't good."

Unfortunately, we've seen this with some of our past clients.

I don't think many clients go into rebranding thinking "we'll just stop at a new look." When this does happen, it's usually an organization that fails to commit enough resources to living out its brand to the fullest. It's sad to see all of the energy that goes into a rebrand wasted because of time, budget, or worst of all, because the organization never really intended to change and improve how it does business.

It doesn't matter how genius your strategy is, how beautiful your new corporate identity may be, or how compelling your new stories, brochures, or website may be. If your company can't stand behind the rebrand and live up to the promises that your brand makes, your brand will quickly stand for something you didn't envision: deception.

1

WINDOW DRESSING
A FAKE FACADE
TO COVER UP A
POOR REPUTATION

2

A FRESH FACE
IMPROVING THE
IMAGE / AWARENESS
OF A STRONG FIRM

3

TOTAL OVERHAUL
COMMITTED TO
IMPROVING BOTH
INSIDE & OUT

4

JUST BECAUSE?
REBRANDING YOUR
FIRM BECAUSE
YOU CAN

A brand that fails to live up to its promise is a LIE.

The reality is, a brand that fails to live up to its promise is a lie.

Sound harsh? It may be, but that's the truth. You've seen this in play before:

"Thank you for calling XYZ Mobile. Please enter your 14-digit account number followed by the pound sign. Your call is very important to us. Please continue to hold for the next available customer service representative."

The minutes tick by. You're drowning in easy listening hold music, interrupted every 15 seconds by the same "your call is very important to us" message.

After what seems like an eternity, a customer service rep mumbles, "Thank you for calling XYZ Mobile. My name is Roberta. Can you please verify your 14-digit account number?"

(Uh, okay.) Sure, it's 3-4-2 ...

"Thank you, can you please verify the last four digits of your social security number?"

(Grrr.) Uh, yes. It's ...

"Thank you..." (silence) "I'm sorry, our computers are really slow today." (Right, like it's just today.) "Okay, what can I do for you today?"

I'm going to be in Mexico next week. I just want to be sure my phone and email will work while I'm away. Can you help me with that?

"I'm sorry sir, I'm customer support. I'll need to transfer you to customer service to assist with this need. May I transfer you now?"

(Sigh.) Okay, thanks ...

The phone rings through to the customer service department...

"Thank you for calling XYZ Mobile. Please enter your 14-digit account number followed by the pound sign..."

Regardless of what you thought of this brand or their service before this call, they've demonstrated very little interest in you as a customer during this interaction—haven't they?

Second approach: A fresh face on a great place.

Putting a "fresh face" on your company may sound like a similar approach to the "window dressing" example. The crucial difference here is that with this approach, the company is already known and well respected by its current clients.

So why would a company that's already known and respected want to update its image? Chances are that the company's visual identity has become dated and the appearance of its brand may be a detractor as new prospects compare them to the competition.

In the end, companies pursuing this rebranding approach often want to better showcase their company as fresh, relevant, and cutting edge. And most importantly, they already have the chops to back it up.

If all your organization needs to do is "dust-off" its image, great things can happen quickly.

Consider the UPS brand update in 2003. Their primary service had not changed in practice. They remained an international player in the shipping business. They were known for their approachable and courteous delivery drivers. (And their male drivers were known for their shorts.)

Unfortunately, their previous logo (designed in 1961 by design legend Paul Rand) was becoming, practically speaking, a bit dated. While the colors and typography were nearly timeless, the "bow" represented a hand-tied string around a package. UPS hadn't allowed string around their packages for years.

What followed was a logo and overall brand update. The new identity was simple and looked "fast" (more befitting of their racing sponsorships). In addition, their new slogan, "What can brown do for you" quickly became part of the public lexicon.

UPS was already a strong, well-respected company, but its brand refresh helped put a new face on a great place and lifted them to even greater success in the shipping business.

Third approach: Total brand overhaul, inside and out.

Companies that completely overhaul their brands must be committed to change, both inside the organization, and in how they are perceived from the outside. When an overhaul is done well, every possible brand touch point is examined thoroughly, asking "how could we make this touch point better?"

Rebranding at this level can be a long, expensive, and challenging undertaking, but when done well, is well worth the investment. This type of holistic approach is the one I can always stand firmly in favor of.

This type of rebranding is also the easiest to spot. You can literally see a wounded organization arise from the ashes of its previous self. Internally, you can spot happy employees who rally around what the brand stands for; externally, you can see the evidence of where the brand plans to grow. This is the type of energy we saw in the late 90s when Steve Jobs returned to Apple, reinvigorating the leadership, product line, and public perception of the company.

Sometimes an organization undergoes a rebrand solely to overcome internal issues. It can be as innocuous as a merger—two corporate cultures need to be melded into something new. Or it may be an issue such as a corporate downsizing or public relations problem. Quick-serve restaurants go through these issues all the time. Regardless of whether or not it was true, the Wendy's "fingertip in the chili" story sent shivers down the backs of patrons nationwide. Wendy's isn't the only fast-food giant to suffer from these types of food-quality scares. Often the fastest type of response to these issues is a campaign restating the company's commitment to fresh ingredients.

Is there a fourth approach?

Occasionally, a beloved company that enjoys a fantastic position in the market has no internal or any obvious problems in the marketplace, but chooses to rebrand anyway. This can be a dicey move. Think about the recent rebrandings of Tropicana, Pepsi, and Nickelodeon. Each already enjoyed well-respected market positions, and all of the rebrands were met with some initial criticism.

The only logical explanation for this type of rebranding is that the company felt it needed an update in one area or another. They all saw opportunities to make improvements or they wouldn't have undergone the process. I have a hard time believing that any business rebrands "just because." So for my money, there are still only three reasons for rebranding.

That said, if you're truly falling into the fourth category of "updating your brand just because," let's face it: your company must have money to burn. Congratulations!

Which approach will you take?

If you're considering a rebrand, it's essential that you focus on each and every touch point of the brand, not the least of which is how the brand performs and delivers on its product, service, or promises.

The goal is not only to develop the workings for a great brand, but also to create a clear picture of how to live out that brand on a daily basis. With the guidance of a positioning document, a rebrand will lead to authentic improvements for a company, both internally and externally. But much like a playbook, if you don't go back to the document on a regular basis, it's easy to be tempted to cut corners and forsake much of the intended brand architecture.

Be intentional in how you proceed with a rebrand. Be true to your vision, and avoid the "window dressing" approach. Employees and clients alike can sniff out a brand that's not being true to itself. And you can count on them knowing it "ain't good."

Homework:

☐ When do brands get it right? When do they get it wrong?

☐ Think about a company that has rebranded. Did your perception of the company improve following the rebrand? Which have fallen short?

☐ Do you know of companies that fail to deliver on their promises? Have you stopped using their products, services, or brands?

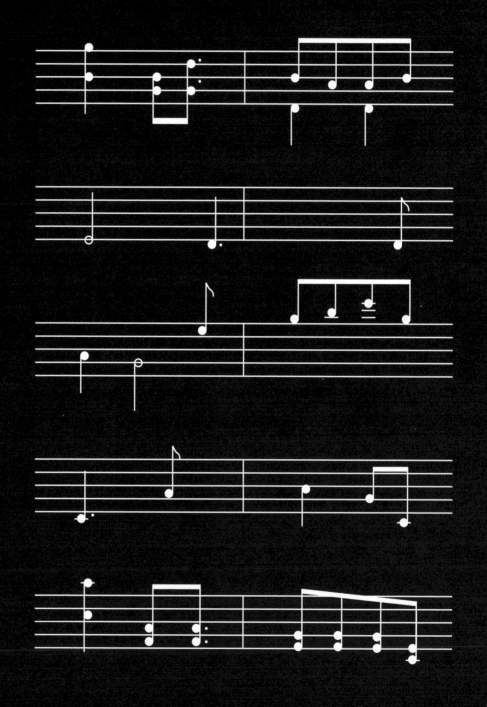

CHAPTER SEVEN

An Ownable Voice

More often than not, a rebrand doesn't go much further than skin deep, even verbally speaking. You need to create a "voice" that is as unique and ownable as your new "look."

"It's not technique—
it's what you have
to say."

—Les Paul

When most companies think of a rebrand, they probably picture a new look and feel, a new logo, and hopefully a new positioning strategy. Maybe (if they're really thinking ahead) they'll consider a new tagline or even a new company name.

But more often than not, a rebrand doesn't go much further than skin deep, even verbally speaking. When the corporate website and marketing materials get spruced up, how many brands take the time to rethink the copy on the pages, the headlines, the voicemail messages, or the instructions on the online forms? Very few.

Do you remember when you were in grade school? If your school was anything like ours, when the weather didn't cooperate during recess, we had to stay in our classrooms and play games. One of the games was the telephone game. It went something like this:

Everyone sat in a big circle. The teacher would whisper a phrase in the first student's ear. Their job was to remember the phrase as closely as possible, and repeat it to their neighbor. Of course, as the message went around the circle, it got more and more distorted. Sometimes by the time it reached the end of the circle, the original phrase was completely changed. At best, the underlying message may have been maintained, but more often than not, the intended meaning became just as jumbled and unrecognizable as the original phrase.

Every now and then, a phrase would make it all the way through, unscathed. Why would some phrases work well, and others completely fail? There's a good chance that it had a lot to do with the original message itself. Phrases that would make it all the way around the circle were usually short, concise, and simple. Of course, it didn't hurt if the phrase was humorous or unexpected. Short and to-the-point phrases promised much better outcomes around the telephone game circle.

Corporate messages are no different. Headlines, taglines, elevator speeches, and mission or vision statements are the building blocks of what we call a brand's voice.

Your brand's voice isn't a one liner. It's not a programmed way of speaking either. Voice, however, is very intentional. Many young brands make the mistake of coming off either too lock-step in their voice, or have an innate fear that having a scripted baseline for communications will yield a fake-sounding brand. These are two extreme views, and neither makes for a very compelling experience.

One of my favorite "quirky" brands is the email marketing company Emma.

Emma has a clear idea of what they want their brand to both look and sound like. Their voice is casual and friendly, and there is almost always an undertone of humor in their messaging. Every communication from Emma lets the reader feel like he or she is sharing an inside joke.

Does this voice work for very serious, highly critical professionals? Probably not. But it does help a software company sound very human and personal. Not an easy feat for a service that is sold almost entirely online and over the phone.

Stop for a moment to think about how a one-paragraph bio for an average software executive might sound. Now take a look at the bio for one of Emma's founders:

Bio: Will Weaver

Will Weaver is one of the co-founders here at Emma. He sets the design direction and coordinates all things technological. He is also very tall. It was Will who proposed one afternoon in late 2001, over assorted coffee drinks, that a company be started, one that might create a web-based service to help businesses of all shapes and sizes. Being the tallest person at the table, others felt inclined to listen and, during pauses in conversation, to nod vigorously. Before helping start Emma, Will served as the Web Director for Nashville-based custom-publisher Hammock Publishing and as a founding member of Smallbusiness.com. Will is a graduate of The University of The South, known in more casual circles as Sewanee.

As you may notice, this bio still drops in some important, corporate details about Will, but it does so in a very non-traditional style. We can find his title, his role, schooling, as well as background. What's missing, however, is a fluffed up paragraph of unimportant job descriptions.

What makes Emma's voice so great is they know not only who they are, but also who they're talking to. Advertising and design firms are a large part of their potential client base, and they know what it takes to stand out to companies that specialize in helping other companies stand out. It has to be fresh, unexpected, and consistent.

Every year Emma holds a call-for-entries for a non-profit they can donate their services to. Here's a snippet from their request for entries:

> "Know a small, deserving non-profit in your neighborhood? Think they could do even more incredible work with the help of a free Emma account? Are people giving you funny looks because you keep saying 'yes' to your computer?

> Well then, question-answering friend, it's that time of year to nominate a non-profit for the Emma 25. It's an annual Emma tradition where we team up with you to award free Emma service to 25 non-profits around the world, plus an additional 25 groups in cities Emma calls home—Nashville, Portland, Denver, and Austin …"

Even when extending their brand to a social cause, Emma maintains their quirky voice. For more information about Emma, check out MyEmma.com, and be sure to read some of the deeper content for some real copywriting gems.

Cover up the logos.

So does a brand have to maintain a quirky or humorous tone to be memorable? Of course not. The off-beat language used at Emma is just one example. Your brand voice may be friendly, knowledgeable, technical, or very serious. Is your language as differentiated as your positioning? Here's one way to tell:

Open up your website next to your competitor's website. Cover up the logos and begin reading. If they sound like either firm could have said it, you've probably got some work to do.

Find a voice you can own.

Practically speaking, how does a brand begin to develop its own voice? Start simple, with something we've already talked about— your brand positioning document.

Take a look at your audience section. Think of a few of your current clients in each audience category. What types of things do they like? What type of voice might they respond best to? Are you speaking to tweens, Millennials, Gen-Xers, or Baby Boomers?

In finding the right voice, don't feel like you can't use certain styles. Scientists may respond just as well to humor as ad agency executives, but the technique may require a different approach. The key is to find the style of voice that will best communicate with your client base.

Also consider how you want your brand to be perceived. If

you're interested in maintaining a sense of reverence and respect, overt humor or playful copy is probably the wrong direction to take your voice.

After considering audience and perception, think about how your competitors sound.

Some industries become parodies of themselves, especially when it comes to "voice." Picture how many auto dealer ads blend together. Even their on-lot shtick of raised hoods, balloons, streamers, and neon window paint scream, "What's it gonna take to get you in this car today!?"

We often joke, "You know I wasn't even looking for a new car, but when I drove by and saw the balloons on your lot, I just had to stop in!"

If every car dealership in town has a twangy, high-pitched, yell-at-the-screen voice, perhaps a professional-sounding woman would stand out in the crowd.

If your auto dealer made you feel like they'd help you research and find the ideal vehicle for your family, wouldn't that feel different than having the latest sale shouted at you in a screechy panic?

That type of approach is what we call an "ownable voice." It would be unique to the brand if no other auto dealer was positioning itself as your "expert guide." It's a voice that over time would be closely associated with that brand, and that brand alone.

Put your voice into practice.

After you've thought through your audience and style, write down all the things about your voice direction that you've decided on.

Let's go back to our auto dealer example.

Let's call them "Safari Motors."

Safari Motors has chosen a calm, expert voice—a cross between a surgeon and a zoologist. The voice is helpful, guiding, and professional. For verbal ads, they've decided to use female voice talent whenever possible. Their "voice statement" is as follows:

Safari Motors voice: The professional and knowledgeable experts to help you find the perfect car for your family.

Check your work: If you've done this well and have been honest with yourself, your voice statement and your brand essence should pair together like a gourmet dish and the perfect glass of wine.

Start making headlines.

Armed with your voice statement, you might take a stab at writing headlines.

Be warned, this isn't as easy as you might hope. Most business owners who are not trained writers are just about as skilled at writing headlines as they are at writing mission statements. Most novices will fall into the trap of writing headlines that are strikingly similar to competitors without even trying. This is a great spot to enlist the help of a professional copywriter. Trust me, it's money well spent.

Here are a few ideas a professional copywriter might come up with for Safari Motors:

"It's easy to spot a deal; unfortunately finding your perfect car isn't."

"We'll help you explore your options. Safari Motors."

"Shouldn't finding the perfect car be just as easy as finding a good deal?"

Writing great copy isn't easy, but there's a certain level of "the first one has been done for you" that translates. If you're feeling uneasy about having a professional rewrite hundreds of pages of copy on your website, contract with them to write the most important and the most highly trafficked pages. After that, you may feel more comfortable in following along in a similar voice to flesh out the remaining elements or pages. A few sample headlines probably aren't enough to get the hang of the voice, but a few essential website pages may be. It's all a matter of comfort level, and how quickly you can adapt to your copywriter's style.

Elevator speech.

Your elevator speech is basically the intersection of your brand voice and your brand essence. It's often used in networking circles (as we illustrated previously) and should be brief enough to get across in no more than three sentences.

We often encourage clients to break their two- or three-sentence elevator speech into a tease with a payoff. If your tease isn't enough to draw out a few questions, that person probably isn't much of a prospect to begin with. However, if your elevator speech can be shortened into a memorable, compelling one-liner, that will do just fine.

Going back to our auto dealer example, here are two different ways a Safari Motors salesperson might phrase their elevator speech:

(One-liner)

> … and what is it you do?

> "I'm a family fit specialist at Safari Motors. I help families identify the best vehicle, and then we help them find the best deal."

(Tease)

> … I'm a customer sales rep at the local bank, how about you?

> "I help families find their perfect vehicle with some tools you'd expect, and one that you wouldn't."

> … uh, and what tool would that be?

> "ME! I only get paid if I help my clients find the best fit and the best deal for them."

See how that's a different approach and how it might yield a different response from a potential client?

Of course, the teaser line may be the perfect segue into a deeper discussion about your experience, teamwork, or approach. Longer conversations should be somewhat scripted as well (using a bullet point approach), but the conversation should maintain a natural flow, and not feel staged or stiff.

Your tagline:
saying what's best for you.

Unlike most of the other voice and copy elements we've discussed so far, the tagline is not something you absolutely must have. Certain brands are better suited for using taglines than others. Sometimes the corporation may have one, but the product or service lines do not, and sometimes it's the other way around.

Who has a "great" tagline?

Everyone is probably familiar with some famous B2C or retail taglines: "Just do it." "Improving home improvement." "Like a rock."

But what about B2B or professional services taglines? Those admittedly are a little harder to come by, but a few strong ones include:

"Welcome to the human network."—Cisco

"Better living through chemistry."—DuPont

"Intel Inside."—Intel

"This is MoFo." – Morrison Foerster (a shorthand of this international law firm's name doubles as its "tagline," too). Now that's a brand promise!

Does your firm need a tagline?

This really comes down to your company's messaging strategy and how you would like your story to be told. The most awkward use of a tagline, in my opinion, is when you can't really tell which line is the payoff to the copy, which is the tagline, and which is the corporate sign off.

In other words, some brands get stuck in the rut of tagging everything—the headline, the body copy, the logo, and even the call-to-action.

The best recommendation I can make is to think through how you might want to use a tagline before you spend too much time writing it, let alone paying someone else to write it for you.

An unclear messaging or tagline strategy quickly becomes confusing—not just to your audience, but also to the team trying to assemble the communication pieces.

As a young art director in the late 90s, I was working for a small advertising agency. I struggled with developing ads for one of our clients because they suffered from acute tagline-itis. It made my job to design and layout their ads very difficult.

Here's a sample of what I'd be required to do. We'd have to design a print ad to run in our local newspaper. Typically we ran black-and-white ads that were 1/4 to 1/8 of a page or smaller. Although they were not giant, full-page print ads, they were still expensive to run. Space was limited, but for a typical ad, we'd need to include the following:

Headline—something clever to stop the reader

Subhead—a payoff to the headline

A photo or graphic—lifestyle images tying into the headline or product, and occasionally both

Body copy—the "meat" of the message, typically one to three paragraphs

Call-to-action—call today or visit our location, or worse yet, a list of locations

Logo—brand identity

Tagline—a few words locked up with the logo

A member of XYZ Company—often below the tagline

Contact info—phone, URL, etc.

Membership bugs—some services/products required these items

Disclaimer—legalese as-needed.

Now if that wasn't bad enough, occasionally we'd try to build momentum with campaign-style messaging. One campaign I

Which message in your ad is *most* important?

(stock lifestyle photo goes here)

And will we ever find it? Yikes.

Lorem ipsum is often used as placeholder text in the body of an ad or layout. Typically the final text that is dropped in is either shorter or longer than intended. It's always best to start with the actual text, then layout second. Here's really where the "meat" of your message will probably go, so don't lose it in too much text.

Call to Action: Stop by any location for details

- **Location Number One**
- **Location Number Two**
- **Location Number Three**

Logo Goes Here

your tagline here.

800-000-0000   **www.visitourreallylongweburl.com**

Disclaimer: Here's all the reasons that you won't ever actually be able to qualify for this offer, again probably way too much text. Sorry legal department—but is this really necessary?

Official Service of the Home Team.   Member:

DOES YOUR AD SUFFER FROM ACUTE TAGLINE-ITIS?

was involved in revolved around being the official sponsor of a community program. So in addition to the laundry list above, we had to include the campaign tagline and a sponsorship sign-off of "the official service of the local team." After demonstrating before and after versions of the ads, I was finally able to convince my agency and client to shed a few of those items for future campaign pieces.

Another example of unclear messaging that you've probably seen is Intel. Don't get me wrong—Intel has done a fabulous job of branding itself. They even use chimes along with their tagline "Intel Inside." You may not really understand what the "Intel Inside" is all about, but you probably know it's good for your laptop.

However, if I were running Dell or HP, I'd probably request that Intel tone down its sign-off message. The Intel graphics and chimes often interrupt the feel and flow of the advertiser's message. Do you think most consumers remember the computer ads, or the Intel chimes? Probably the latter. Sure, Intel pays for that time and is probably helping these other companies alleviate their ad spend. And if you're able to share your media costs with one of your suppliers, it's not such an awful trade-off—or is it?

Do you know who else uses Intel chips? Apple. So why don't we see the Intel clip at the end of Apple's commercials? It's simple. Apple understands the value of their TV advertisement time. They probably wouldn't be interested in sharing the spotlight with Intel, even if it means footing the entire bill for their ads. Don't be surprised if an Intel logo makes a cameo in a future Apple spot, but if you hear the chimes, you'll know something has shifted over at Apple.

Make a tagline reduction.

Let's consider how to create a tagline. Let's first assume you've thought through how you want the pacing of your messages to work, and you feel a tagline would be a beneficial addition. Second, let's assume you have a strong positioning document, a powerful brand essence, and a compelling elevator pitch. If so, you're ready to create a tagline reduction.

In gourmet cooking, some of the most flavorful sauces are created through a process called reduction. It slowly cooks away the excess liquid by evaporating the mixture down to only the remaining ingredients. It yields a thicker and more flavorful sauce.

If you think of your positioning document, brand essence, and elevator pitch as your ingredients, your tagline goal should be to decide which "flavors" of your brand you want to call attention to.

In the case of more descriptive brands, like Best Buy, your tagline goal may be more inspirational—for example their previous tagline, "Turn on the fun." In the case of a less descriptive brand name, you may choose a tagline that describes or defines your USP. In short, the tagline should describe the most unique elements of your brand.

For many of our clients, if their brand essence is spot-on, it either becomes the platform for writing their tagline, or becomes the tagline itself. Typically the brand essence contains the right idea, but it is intended for an internal audience, so don't be frustrated if you need to rethink how to phrase it to have it work as a tagline. Here again, you may want to enlist the services of a professional copywriter. A skilled writer can help you distill your USP into a marketable phrase for a memorable tagline.

In the case of our imaginary auto dealer, a few possible taglines could include:

Safari Motors. Discover a new experience. (inspirational)

Safari Motors. Accelerate your search. (problem solving)

Safari Motors. A *lot* of help. (silly pun)

Safari Motors. You've found your navigator. (emotional)

Safari Motors. Working with us is a trip. (fun)

Can you think of a few other tagline concepts for Safari Motors? What are a few descriptive options? How about another emotional direction? How would another inspirational tagline sound?

Mission statements.

We've already talked about my usual displeasure with mission and vision statements, so I'll stay off the soap box for now.

However, a much better time to write a mission statement is after you've really dug into your brand voice. It's not that you wouldn't be able to talk about what your company does and why it matters without your newfound voice. The problem is, if you try to write your mission before you carve out your brand voice, your mission may not sound like your brand.

If you've ever written a mission statement before you developed a brand voice, you'll probably see what I'm talking about. So at the very least, treat that pre-voice mission statement as the scaffolding and build the right mission statement around it— complete with your brand voice to give it that unique flavor.

Who needs a vision statement?

If you have all of these other tools, why would you choose to have a separate vision statement? Let's explore a few possible reasons.

A mission statement focuses on who you are, what you do, and why it should matter. A vision statement is more of a future facing, or even aspirational, statement.

MISSION
- SPECIFIES WHO YOU ARE & WHAT YOU DO
- GOES BEYOND COMMITMENT TO QUALITY
- DRIVEN BY YOUR VOICE & POSITIONING
- ANSWERS: "WHY DO WE MATTER?"

VISION
- DRIVEN BY YOUR GOALS
- ASPIRATIONAL
- FUTURE-FACING
- ANSWERS: "WHERE ARE WE GOING?"

The mission statement for our auto dealer could sound something like this:

> "At Safari Motors, our mission is to be a guiding lighthouse to our clients in a sea of sales-focused sharks. We help families find the best deals on only the vehicles that are the best fit for their lifestyle using the best technologies and tools ... and we're willing to stake our reputation on our high-tech, high-touch promises. If we can't deliver, we don't expect them to buy from us."

It's a pretty compelling statement about how Safari Motors plans to do business on a daily basis, but it leaves out a few details about where they hope that approach will take them. The vision statement expands upon those details:

> "Our vision is for Safari Motors to be the most highly rated auto dealership in the tri-state area. Because our approach is different than just pushing deals out the door, we will probably never sell the most cars, and that's okay. Only by sticking to our values and demonstrating the benefit of our one-of-a-kind approach to client education and guidance will we become one of the Top 10 dealerships in the tri-state area in overall sales."

How will you set your vision? Going back to your positioning document, what were your overall goals? What is driving you to get there? What does the future look like for your brand? With your mission as direction, where are you aiming to hit?

Go find your voice.

As you can see, there are many elements that go into developing a great, ownable voice for your brand. Frankly, it's an exercise that many brands just don't take the time to do well. Given that fact, developing a brand voice is a terrific opportunity for you to further differentiate your professional services firm.

Homework:

☐ Does your firm pass the "cover up the logos" test?

☐ How would you describe your company's voice?

☐ Would a tagline help guide your voice? Try making a tagline reduction.

☐ Do you have a mission?

☐ What is your vision?

CHAPTER EIGHT

Corporate Identity 101: How to Develop, Use, & Protect Great Trademarks

Developing a powerful corporate identity system for your professional services firm is more complex than just designing a cool logo.

"Check yo self before you wreck yo self."

—O'Shea Jackson,
aka Ice Cube

By now you've established what you intend your brand to be known for in the marketplace. You've got a rock-solid positioning document that outlines your business goals and objectives. You understand what makes your brand different. You have a memorable elevator speech. And you've developed a unique, ownable voice for your brand.

If you've been able to keep nodding to all of those statements, you have built a solid foundation for what is coming next. We are finally at the stage where the branding exercise begins to express itself visually. Now is the time to begin building (or recreating) your corporate identity.

Like much of what we've covered so far, when it comes to creating your corporate identity, engaging a well-respected branding or design firm will be a wise investment. We'll find out as we continue just how complex this step in the process can be.

My neighbor is an artist ...

Just because your spouse, nephew, or neighbor has a "flair for the artistic" doesn't mean he or she is going to understand how to develop a great logo or corporate identity system. As the cornerstone of all your future marketing efforts, you owe it to your company, your employees, and your clients to do this well. Unless, of course, your spouse, nephew, or neighbor is an experienced branding or design professional. But even then, be sure he or she is being fairly compensated and is truly involved in the process. You'll get the best work from a professional who is fully engaged in the process.

What is a trademark?

A trademark can be a design, symbol, color, shape, or sound used to identify a product or service. The Intel chimes, the words Coca-Cola, and the Nike swoosh are all examples of trademarks.

For our purposes, we'll discuss what makes a good trademark for a professional services firm. A trademark should tell the buyer two things: who is providing a given product or service, and perhaps more importantly, that the provider is associating their name and reputation with the quality and performance of that product or service.

A trademark protects the public by distinguishing what product or service is provided by whom. This idea of avoiding confusion is at the heart of trademark law. For example, if I wanted to sell ham sandwiches as McDonald's Ham Sandwiches, I'd likely be denied a federal or state trademark registration and I'd expose myself to some infringement liability from McDonald's Corporation.

However, if I'm opening an accounting practice called McDonald's Tax Prep, I'm far less likely to confuse consumers since my accounting service is in a different channel of trade than a fast food restaurant. (Of course, McDonald's still may take legal action against my accounting practice.)

Types of trademarks.

From a technical perspective, there are several categories of potential trademarks:

Generic—Generic terms or nouns are not protectable trademarks. For instance, you can't call your firm "Architecture Firm" and hope to trademark it.

Descriptive—Descriptive names would include someone's

name, plus a generic name of their product or service, like "Miles Design." These marks are sometimes more challenging to protect, but can be trademarked once they have developed a reputation as a recognizable name for that particular service.

Suggestive—Suggestive marks may hint at a generic term, but take a more creative approach. "Dunkin' Donuts" is an example of a suggestive mark.

Arbitrary—Arbitrary marks use a word or phrase completely unrelated to the product or service. These marks are often the easiest to protect. Think of Apple, Red Bull, and Target.

Fanciful—Fanciful marks are often made-up words or phrases. Fanciful marks are often used with food and beverage brands to allude to the sound or flavor of the food they represent. Think of the sound you hear when you open a can of Pepsi.

What is the role of a trademark?

One of the most common mistakes companies make while developing trademarks is trying to use their company name or logo to describe what their company is, does, or creates. However, as we already mentioned, these descriptive marks are weak trademarks.

Historically, as professional services businesses add new partners, it's not uncommon to add the latest partner's last name to the name of the practice. Over time, this is often reduced to a simplified "shorthand" of the mark.

For example, Johnson, Jackson, Jones, and Smith might be referred to as "Johnson Smith" or simply, "JJJS." If all variations of the trademark aren't federally registered, this inconsistent use may begin to weaken the trademark. In addition, the firm can get lost in the "alphabet soup." How many professional services brands can you think of that go by three or four letter nicknames?

Of course, there are examples of such shorthands that work very well. IBM, AT&T, and UPS are all examples of big, successful corporations that have successfully branded themselves with three-letter trademarks. However, these firms have been in business for decades and have spent millions to help you keep their letters straight. Unless you're planning to spend that kind of money on marketing, you'll probably be better off avoiding a three-letter trademark altogether.

Let's look at another example. A new company settles on "Industrial Solutions Company" as its brand name and sets its logomark in all black, capital letters with Arial or Times New Roman.

This is problematic for several reasons. First, neither the name nor the design is particularly special. Such a "generic" mark isn't impossible to register, but it's more challenging to work with than a more distinctive mark. Second, the name is so ubiquitous that it leaves most of its potential clients in the dark. In addition to being difficult to register, mundane, and generic, the name isn't fun to say or the least bit memorable. Think of all of the similarly named companies: Industry Services Corporation, Industrial Services LLC, International Solutions Co., etc.

On the other hand, one of these similar-sounding companies, Industrial Services Corp., for example, might decide that their logomark should include trucks, repairmen, and a giant wrench to make clear exactly what they do. However, once they add design-build capabilities, how will they represent this service in their trademark? Add an icon of a compass?

Apple, of course, is the polar opposite of this example. Their logomark is a simple, silhouetted apple design. Neither the brand name nor the mark describes what they do. In fact, the trademark is based on a FRUIT—perhaps the farthest thing possible from technology!

However, the name is simple and unexpected for a computer company. The trademark is also clean and easily recognizable. It works well large, small, silk-screened, embossed on products, and across various digital media. What makes the Apple brand engaging goes well beyond the simple trademark, but the Apple word mark and design mark are the cornerstones of Apple's corporate identity.

Like Apple, you want to shoot for a trademark that is memorable, distinctive, easy to spell, and fun to say. Practice saying your company name aloud. Does it sound strange? Does it roll trippingly off the tongue? Does it sound like a competing brand name?

A great brand name and trademark is working the hardest for its owner when its only role is to uniquely identify the brand it represents.

What is a logo?

A logo (or more correctly, perhaps, in legalese, a design mark) is a combination of words and distinctive graphics, set in a particular color, typeface, and orientation, intended to identify particular goods or services.

The logo is often the cornerstone of the corporate identity system for any brand. While some brands may have multiple logos (such as corporate logos and product or sub-brand logos), and much of what we're discussing may apply to both, we're mainly focusing our recommendations on the qualities of a singular, corporate logo.

In design terms, logotype and logomark are two different things;

however, they can both serve as trademarks, either separately or together. Think of Target's bullseye design. The type can be considered the "logotype," and the design can be considered the "logomark." Both may be protected as individual trademarks, but together they are protected as well (as the combined logo and trademark).

The late, world-renowned designer Paul Rand was best known for his iconic logo designs including UPS, Colorforms, IBM, ABC, and Cummins. While Rand was famous for his simple, beautiful design approach, he was also known for his no-nonsense approach. Speaking to the role of a logo, Paul Rand said:

"A logo is a flag, a signature, an escutcheon.

A logo doesn't sell (directly), it identifies.

A logo is rarely a description of a business.

A logo derives its meaning from the quality of the thing it symbolizes, not the other way around.

A logo is less important than the product it signifies; what it means is more important than what it looks like...it shows you care."

In short, your trademark or logo should be less concerned with describing your product or service, and more focused on identifying your product or service.

Armed with these legal basics, how should you get started with creating your trademark?

First things first—do your research. With all of the online tools available today, there's no excuse for not performing at least a cursory clearance search to make sure something similar isn't being used by someone else.

Many logo designers have access to various member-supported websites such as Logo Lounge, which is an archive of thousands of logos, cataloged by keyword by the designers who created the marks. Even a basic Google search can help uncover potentially similar marks. Considering a scorpion trademark? Try doing a web search for "scorpion logos" before you get stung.

As you're considering your name, think about your future website domain as well. If you're changing your name or starting a new business, search for available URLs. Ideally, if it's a for-profit business, you'll want to look for available dot com names, Twitter handles, and more. This is another quick way to figure out if anyone else is using your intended trademark, and if so, how.

Once you're ready to go beyond a cursory search, you can have your attorney do an "official" federal trademark search.

Trade names and infringement considerations.

On the flip side, registering a trade name at the state level requires only that the company name is slightly different from any other trade name on file in that state. Often a one-word difference is enough to register a trade name. This doesn't mean, however, that you won't open yourself up to a lawsuit, because the standards for obtaining a trade name are different from those used for trademark infringement analysis.

Put another way, just because you're able to register a business name with the state, doesn't mean you'll be able to protect that same name as a trademark. Consult an experienced intellectual property attorney before finalizing the use of your company name as your trademark.

What is corporate identity?

Corporate identity is everything that visually identifies your brand. It's a system of logos and trademarks, graphics, images, typefaces, corporate color schemes, materials, packaging, and textures. In effect, it's a system that creates unity across all of your brand's touch points—from your logo to your website, to your brochures and contracts. Most successful brands have a brand guidelines document or a corporate identity standards manual that serves as a prescriptive guide for how to create new marketing materials while staying consistent with the overall corporate identity system.

What makes a good identity?

A good identity uniquely identifies a company's goods or services. It needs to be different from the competition, yet familiar enough to be recognized as a particular type of company.

Luckily, you won't exactly be starting from *scratch*. Your positioning brief and brand voice will be valuable guideposts in directing how to approach your corporate identity. If you follow the recommendations in the positioning document, chances are good that the final identity will be authentic. In addition to the "tone" direction the positioning document may provide, an important element to consider is how and where your audience is most likely to interact with and experience the brand.

For example, an industrial maintenance company may have the most visual exposure on its fleet of service vehicles, whereas a professional services company may have the greatest exposure on its website.

Taking these points of interaction into account will help guide your team toward any special considerations. Will the identity ever need to be large? Does it need to be very small? Are there any other special considerations, such as one-color printing or embroidery for apparel? One recent client of ours was concerned about how their corporate identity would appear on the side of a race car they were sponsoring.

How to hire the right logo designer.

Within the graphic design community, work that pushes the bounds of style and technique is often celebrated for its beauty and design aesthetics alone. And in a world where designers judge the design work of other designers, some of the award-winning pieces may not have actually been successful in the real world as of yet. Be sure to find a design or branding partner who prioritizes your business goals over their aesthetic preferences. After all, an award-winning identity system that is ineffective is not doing its job.

While appropriate style considerations should come into play while considering your brand's audience, look for a partner whose portfolio of work matches up with your goals. For instance, our identity work tends to lean on the clean side. Keep in mind how the identity is most likely to be used, and you're more likely to wind up with an authentic identity system that is built for performance. As one of my favorite design professors used to say, "The best identity system lets everything reflect unity, not just blind uniformity. Each piece should look like it's part of a family, but the family shouldn't all look like identical twins!"

What should your trademark look like?

While it should be pretty obvious, I'll go ahead and say this anyway: Don't copy any existing trademark or logo. Besides the fact that it's unethical and illegal to duplicate another company's intellectual property, the "lesser crime" of mimicking another company's identity is just not smart. Remember, the goal of your trademark is to avoid confusion in the marketplace and to uniquely identify your product or service. Using the same color, typeface, or concept as your competition or any other popular trademark is a very poor way to accomplish this.

Above all else, you should strive to make your logo original and distinctive.

Sometimes that can be a formidable challenge.

A logo that feels like it belongs in a certain marketplace may be quickly recognized as a part of that market, but as such, it's just as likely to blend in and go unnoticed. Having a logo that is even "similar" to your competition reduces your chances of standing out.

Consider embracing distinctive colors, shapes, scale, typography, and styling. While being different may feel uncomfortable at first, you'll be pleased when your logo is the "only" logo in your space to look that way.

What colors are overused in your space? Which of your competitors use what colors? Sometimes in very crowded markets, there aren't many colors that aren't being used, but the range of shades, tints, and combinations of colors should afford you nearly infinite possibilities to stake out a one-of-a-kind color palette.

Is there a particular color that you really want to use, even though it's common in your industry? Consider how you could use that color differently or incorporate different complementary colors.

Different styles of logos.

From a design perspective, logos can be categorized as follows:

Logotypes—Logotypes, or "fanciful" marks, are stylized type alone. Think of FedEx, Big Ten, and Google. Often the most successful logotypes use custom-drawn letterforms, or a typeface that has been somewhat customized for the mark. This prevents other firms from being able to easily duplicate the mark. Logotypes often work best in horizontal formats.

Badges—Badge marks are self-contained marks that are flexible on dark or light fields. They can overlay a photograph and still be readable. Many auto manufacturers have badge marks. Think Harley Davidson, Ford, BMW, and Lamborghini. These marks are often circle- or square-shaped, giving them great prominence on a car hood or television commercial.

Mark and type combo—This is one of the most common styles of logo design. A mark and type logo offers flexibility and can be rearranged in a horizontal or vertical stack. Examples include Target, NBC, and Delta Airlines.

Mark only—Very few brands can stand alone as just a mark. It takes years of exposure and millions of dollars in advertising. These are truly iconic brands like Nike and Apple. Occassionally these marks are used as mark and type combinations, but you're most likely to see them used as mark only.

Do I always have to use my logo the same way?

Consistent usage of your trademark is paramount. As you can imagine, a logo that is being used inconsistently is much more difficult to protect and enforce. Even the shape-shifting identity systems used by Nickelodeon, AOL, and Fossil maintain consistent elements throughout. While these brands are in a constant state of flux, they remain easily recognizable and reflect brand consistency. Or as I like to say, they're consistently inconsistent.

SM, TM, ®, and proprietary notices.

Trademark rights arise from use, not registration. Therefore, your mark doesn't have to be "registered" for you to use proprietary notices like the TM (trademark) or SM (service mark), which often are used interchangeably. As long as you're using your logo in commerce, you can include the TM or SM on your logo without any additional legwork. By using a TM or SM, you're claiming, or "giving notice," to customers and competitors that THAT is your mark. However, that only provides a minimum level of protection against infringers of your mark.

The most basic way to formally protect your mark is to apply for a state trademark. Laws vary from state to state, so consult your attorney for the specifics in your area. State trademark applications can often be found online, and filing fees typically cost much less than a federal trademark application. A state registration only protects you in that given state, so if you are offering goods and services across state lines, a federal registration is preferable.

To use the registered trademark symbol, ® or "R-Ball" as it's sometimes called, your trademark must be federally registered. Properly maintained, a federal trademark registration can last for the life of the product or service.

Infringement of a federal mark can open the door to a federal court case.

When applying for a federal trademark registration, you'll need to include either evidence of the use of the mark in interstate commerce, or file an "intent-to-use" application. In addition, you'll be required to submit:

- Information about the owner of the trademark

- A description of the goods or services on which the mark is used

- Samples of the mark if it is a design mark

- A first-use date

- An example of the usage (this will be required in the initial application if you are already using the mark, or later if you file an intent-to-use application)

- The appropriate filing fees for each class of goods and services.

The application process for a federal trademark can be long and arduous—expect it to take at least six months. Complex cases can take a year or longer. Registration is not guaranteed. Don't expect anything to happen too quickly, but once you've got a federally registered trademark, you have yet another asset for your company and your brand. At this point, you can and should begin using the ® symbol in conjunction with your trademark.

How can you protect your trademark?

What's the best way to build and maintain the strength of your trademark? The first (and most overlooked) step is to use it correctly and consistently in text and marketing materials. Think also about how you can distinguish your trademark when you're not able to use it in its graphic form. Perhaps it's always in all capital letters, title case, bold face, italic, a certain color, or different in some other way from the surrounding copy.

You've probably seen brochures, websites or printed advertisements that show the ® after every mention of a product or service. While this isn't necessarily wrong, it can be disruptive for the reader. It's also legally acceptable to only use the appropriate proprietary symbol once per message or page. Often the first appearance of the trademark is the most appropriate place to do this. If it's a website, you may choose to give notice once on every page. On a business card, you'd only need to give notice on one side. In a print ad, once is enough.

For further protection, always use your mark as an adjective, not a noun (e.g., "Xerox copiers" and "Kleenex facial tissues"). These are two pretty well known examples of marks that have become increasingly difficult to protect. Xerox and Kleenex are sometimes used as generic terms for copy machines and facial tissue, yet they are both registered trademarks. If your mark becomes generic, you could lose your exclusive rights to your very own brand name. For obvious reasons, this is a major pitfall that savvy marketers should avoid.

Standards guides and approval processes.

Brand identity standards guides and approval processes are two additional safeguards, which when properly put into place, will help protect your trademarks.

We develop an appropriately sized corporate identity standards guide for our branding clients that outlines proper usage of their trademark, brand colors, typography, and other design elements. For some of our larger clients, we outline the basic structure of their print collateral templates, email signatures, and even the language in some of their marketing materials.

For logo usage, the most important elements are design, clearance, colors, and applications (including what NOT to do). For many logos, we show not only the primary usage, but sometimes also include a shorthand or alternate orientation of the logo for special applications. For example, we may design a nickname mark or vertical version of a long-named, horizontally oriented logo. Of course, we always specify one version that is the preferred mark, so that the alternate version is only used for special needs. (Ideally, both forms of your trademark should be federally registered.) Regardless, be sure the standards guide specifies the design of the logo, including the typeface used, and whether it is a standard font or a customized version.

Another important element of consistent usage, which is often overlooked, is logo clearance. Logo clearance is usually measured as a percentage or ratio of an element of a logo. For example, if the logo is a big X, the clearance around all four sides of the logo may be 1/2 of the height of the X. This ensures that, regardless of how large or small the logo is displayed, it always has the same amount of space around it, relative to the size of the logo itself.

Your standards guide should also spell out flexible yet consistent use of color. Most designers will specify a particular shade of a logo color using the Pantone Matching System, or its parent system, GOE. Pantone colors are communicated as a number, and as a best practice should include the relative color name, such as Pantone 288 Blue. Certain Pantone or other "spot" ink colors may reproduce better across various media than others. Talk with your designer about selecting colors that will not only look great as spot colors, but also will convert nicely to a full-color or four-color (CMYK) printing process, as well as on-screen television and web graphics.

Finally, the standards guide should include examples of proper usage of the logo across various media. Some standards will even include how the logo should be "locked-up" with other graphic page elements, such as a tagline, phone number, call-to-action, or web address. Examples of what not to do also should be included, such as color shifting, rotating, distorting, manipulating, ghosting, or placing a logo over a dark or busy image.

Regardless of how loose or strict your usage policies may be, they won't help protect your brand if nobody is enforcing them. Select someone to sign off on all newly created materials, or at least have several employees share in the review process. An ideal approval process should include a simple checklist of do's and don'ts to maintain brand consistency.

Last but not least, it's essential that your company police the marketplace to ensure that no one is violating your trademarks. You may never need to go much further than a phone call or email, but a simple cease and desist letter from your attorney can be an invaluable next line of defense. At the very least, don't allow violations of your trademark to persist, or it will demonstrate indirectly that you're okay with the violation, which will decrease the strength of your rights moving forward.

Be advised.

Understanding all that goes into a professionally designed logo and corporate identity system underscores our caution against using a friend or ambitious amateur to develop some of the most valuable assets of your brand. Do you think your neighbor or brother-in-law will do a cursory search, or have the know-how to properly assemble a corporate identity standards guide?

With all of the potential issues that may arise from a new identity system—aesthetically, strategically, and legally speaking—weigh your options heavily before cutting corners in this phase of brand development.

Homework:

☐ Is your logo distinctive, unique, and memorable?

☐ Do you use your brand elements consistently?

☐ Has your firm registered any of its trademarks?

☐ Do a basic "cursory search" on your company name using a search engine. Do you see anything of concern?

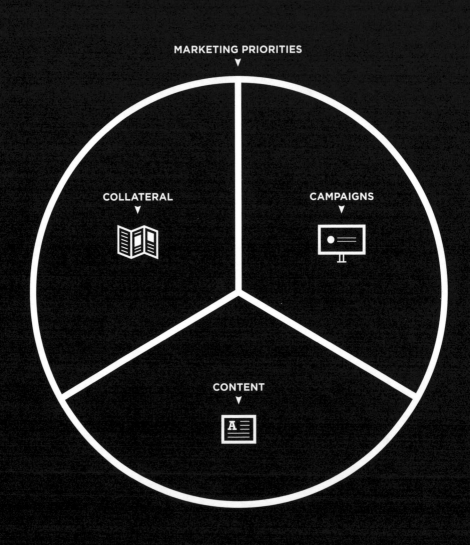

CHAPTER NINE

Collateral, Campaigns, & Content: Brand Touch Points that Work Best for Professional Services Firms

How to determine and prioritize the methods that will work best for you.

> "One day Alice came to a fork in the road and saw a Cheshire cat in a tree. 'Which road do I take?' she asked.
>
> 'Where do you want to go?' was his response.
>
> 'I don't know,' Alice answered.
>
> 'Then,' said the cat, 'it doesn't matter.'"
>
> —Lewis Carroll

If you need a loan, chances are your bank is going to ask you for something to use as collateral. For your bank, collateral is like an insurance policy, showing them that you're good for your word.

Perhaps you've never thought of it this way, but marketing collateral isn't all that different. Collateral is a validation tool that helps back up the story of your capabilities. Your collateral isn't ever going to take the place of face-to-face conversations between your sales team and prospective clients, but great collateral can help your prospects leave those meetings with a sense of security that lasts beyond the conversation. Your collateral should echo your brand messages and feel consistent with your corporate identity and brand standards.

The old joke in the marketing industry is that every new client would start off by declaring, "I need a brochure." Of course, a brochure is seldom the best way to solve a marketing problem. Today it's far more common for new clients to ask for something digital: a website upgrade, a social media strategy, or if you're really cutting edge, a QR code.

The tools have changed, but the questions remain. Do you really need a QR code? Maybe, but how do you determine what to do first?

And more importantly, how can you decide exactly what you need? There is no shortage of options. Your firm will likely discuss the merits of creating business cards, letterhead, additional stationery pieces, brochures, and possibly other printed materials. You may discuss advertising campaigns, and other brand touch points, such as point of purchase, signage, apparel, vehicle graphics, tradeshow materials, direct mail, and ad specialty items. The list of ad specialty items can be overwhelming by itself: hats, umbrellas, ink pens, golf balls, and on, and on, and on.

Intimidated? Don't freak out just yet.

Depending on how large your company is, you may only realistically need a few of the above items. Or if your firm is on the large side, is in start-up mode, or has a hefty outbound marketing approach, you may need far more collateral resources. Carefully consider the purpose of each piece before you begin cranking them out. Just because you have a budget to print 10,000 pocket folders doesn't mean you'll ever actually have a use for 10,000 of them.

Take a step back to carefully consider what collateral your firm really does need. How can you do that?

There are two approaches for prioritizing your collateral needs.

The two approaches we've found most helpful in prioritizing marketing collateral needs are:

1. Marketing priorities.

2. Sales opportunities.

That's probably not a shocking list. Most collateral needs stem from items your marketing team feels are missing or information that could help fill a gap in your sales process.

Marketing priorities.

Start by making a list. Detail every possible piece of marketing collateral need you can think of. After you've created the list, rank every item as either a "1" (essential today), a "2" (soon to be required), a "3" (not essential but could eventually be helpful), or "4" (basically a luxury—unnecessary for now). Then reorder the list so you can see which items you need to address now and which items can wait.

Sales opportunities.

Next, slice up your marketing collateral needs by considering the various stages your prospects go through in your sales process (include your sales and business development staff in this exercise). For most professional services businesses, your prospects probably go through stages something like this: unqualified prospect, qualified lead, active proposal, current client, referral source.

Your method of ranking and qualifying your leads or customer lifecycle may differ from my verbiage above, and that's okay. In fact, it's important to frame this conversation in a way that your team will relate to, so adjust the number of stages and labels appropriately. If you haven't categorized prospects in this way before, the number of stages or names isn't important, just try to keep it simple. Understand that prospects may need different tools and more customized messaging in each stage in order to mature into sales.

For instance, early stage opportunities are often more interested in marketing that excites and inspires. What tools would help you accomplish this?

Other categories, especially late stage opportunities, require more face-to-face time and reassurance tactics. What marketing tools would be most helpful in this instance?

According to Scott McKain, the 2011 Society for Marketing Professional Services (SMPS) National Conference Build Business keynote speaker and author of *Collapse of Distinction*, a recent study shows that only 6 percent of satisfied B2B customers are repeat customers! So don't forget past and current clients. Which marketing tools or tactics would better engage them? My guess is it's not your brochure!

Now make a list of your sales opportunities by stage. This should be similar to your marketing priorities list. Consider which stages are likely to be most impacted by the addition of these tools.

Now compare your two lists. Which items appear to be your top priorities? The biggest win will come from identifying items that are most requested by marketing—items that sales could benefit from as well. Weigh the potential outcomes of doing a few expensive pieces, versus several more affordable items.

At this point, you should have a solid roadmap of which items should have top billing, and which pieces can wait until later.

Collateral best practices.

It would be nearly impossible to write up suggestions for every conceivable piece of collateral. And who really wants to read that book?

Although each situation is different, and the opportunities vary, we do see common patterns among our professional services clients regarding their collateral needs. Let's take a look at some of the most common items discussed.

Color—Across the myriad of printing options, and the various materials and media, color can be an incredibly tricky thing to control. We'll assume at this point that you have standardized your corporate colors as designated Pantone matching system numbers, but that's often not enough to ensure consistency.

Have you ever picked out the perfect paint color for your home only to see that it didn't quite look the same once you slathered it on the wall? Me too. Paint colors have a funny way of shifting based on the surroundings, the lighting in the space, and the surface on which they are applied. Printing inks are very much the same.

So while you may have a "standard" set of Pantone colors in your identity, it always helps to have a sample piece that your printer can use to match. Much like those home improvement store paints, your printer can adjust color mixes to better dial in the perfect shade of your Pantone color. And don't be afraid to ask!

An experienced designer will go out of his or her way to help you with this as well, because it can be pretty embarrassing to have a portfolio full of mismatched print samples. Ask for suggestions for spot colors and any other processes you plan to pursue. Having unique color mixes specified for coated vs. uncoated paper stock can be a huge help, too. In addition, Pantone sells a "bridge" guide that demonstrates how well certain colors translate from spot to process printing. Keep an eye out for potential problems from the beginning, and insist on colors that perform well across all media.

Consistency—Outside of matching colors, consistency in design, rhythm, language, and texture are all things your prospects and clients are likely to respond to. Resist the urge to "switch things up" on every other piece you develop. If you think prospects are getting bored by your consistency, it's probably just you. As we discussed earlier, strive to reflect unity, not blind uniformity.

Business cards—For most of our clients, this is a great place to invest some healthy budget, time, and effort. Aside from your personal appearance and style, little else has as much of a first and lasting impact as your business card. Materials like thick card stock, textured papers, or even metal or plastic can be very impactful. Metallic inks, die-cut shapes, and other specialty processes can also be very memorable.

Our business cards are a little shorter than average, and printed with a matte metallic finish on a rather thick plastic stock. We've sat through many introductory meetings with clients who have fiddled with our card the entire time. They couldn't help it—our business cards create the kind of impact you can't measure. But it's this type of X-factor we want all our clients to enjoy.

Stationery package—Don't be afraid to consider different types of papers and specialty printing processes to help differentiate your stationery package. We've even received compliments on our invoices because of the cool papers we use for our letterhead and envelopes. Clients feel like they're receiving a special package, even when it's actually a bill for our services.

Brochures and other print collateral—Do you really need a company brochure? Think through any print item you think you need and consider if it's something you just think you're supposed to do, or if it will be an asset that will actually get some use. Also, consider at what stage in the sales process a brochure would be most useful, and tailor the messaging to that stage.

Tradeshow displays, presentation kits, and PowerPoint templates—What do all three of these things have in common? In our experience, they usually have too much copy and junk crammed into the space. Treat each of these like a billboard. Fewer words, more sizzle, and memorable concepts!

Presentation materials are common in professional services marketing, but they're usually accompanied by a presenter or salesperson. Don't try to tell the whole story with these pieces. Be sure to leave something to the imagination ... a tease if you will. Don't try to communicate everything at once.

Ad specialties, apparel, and other gear—Similar to your tradeshow display or PowerPoint template, your corporate promotional items should aim to do more with less "stuff." A classy logo and URL on your company umbrella or golf shirt is probably not only better looking, but also far more likely to be used or worn by your client than something featuring a hokey marketing message.

Vehicle graphics, billboards, and other ads—Do you remember the last time you wrote down a phone number you saw on a billboard? Or called the company whose phone number appeared on the truck in front of you? Neither do I. You're wasting an opportunity to provide useful information on a billboard or vehicle if you're listing a giant phone number. There are very few exceptions. Seriously, unless you're a taxi service or have integrated your phone number deeply into your branding, lose the phone number on your vehicles and billboards.

Instead, view billboards and fleet graphics as canvases to echo your brand message or location. Location billboards are highly effective. Vehicle graphics with calls-to-action? Not so much.

Other touch points—Lastly, remember that every touch point you have with an employee, partner, or customer is an opportunity to express your brand message or promote your current campaign. Don't fall into the trap of, "Oh, it's just a parking lot sign—it doesn't have to be that professional." Wrong.

Think about the last time you encountered an unexpected but well-executed brand touch point. Perhaps it was a business card. Or something printed in an unexpected location. Or a message in an unexpected location.

Let's take a look at the business card that Sally Hogshead uses. Sally is a renowned keynote speaker and personal branding consultant. Her business card is oversized, colorful, and interactive. The seven strips on her card reveal messages that relate to her consulting practice, and it's very nicely designed.

"Once you fascinate someone, they become totally focused on your message. So when we were creating our business card for Fascinate, Inc., of course it needed to fascinate people," Sally says. "This business card is an invitation to interact. It immediately captures attention...people love seeing which trigger best describes their personality, hidden underneath that peel-off strip."

When people like Sally really understand the value of their collateral and really get this right, I can't help but smile.

Campaigns.

If you're considering an advertising campaign, regardless of whether it's print, television, outdoor or online, you need to remember two things:

1. Most people are trying to ignore your "interruption tactics" as much as possible.

2. Unless it's really clear what you want someone to remember and what you want them to do, they probably won't remember or do anything.

Look-alike, sound-alike, and me-too messaging in your advertising is a tremendous waste of valuable advertising dollars. You're better off spending zero on advertising than blowing money on imitation messaging.

Remember, your advertising campaigns can change seasonally, annually, or as often as you can afford to try something new. Ad campaigns give you even more freedom to push the expression of your brand within the bounds of your brand standards.

Get creative and come at it from a different angle. If you don't, nobody is going to remember your brand, and certainly not your offer or campaign. Remember, be different, not hokey.

Visually speaking, campaigns give you an opportunity to dress the brand up in something new, without completely throwing away your brand standards. Target, Apple, Intel, and Starbucks do campaigns impeccably well. Always fresh, yet always on point.

It's true that many companies are pulling money from traditional advertising and using those dollars for SEO marketing, social media, and other content marketing opportunities. Whether that makes sense for your situation depends on the factors surrounding your business.

Content marketing.

One of the hottest areas for professional services marketers today is a concept called "content marketing."

As a quick primer, content marketing is the practice of creating valuable content—stories, articles, how-to pieces, testimonials, blogs, white papers, case studies, videos, infographics, e-books, and more—to help tell your brand's story.

Joe Pulizzi knows a thing or two about content marketing. He and Newt Barrett co-authored one of the first popular books on the subject, *Get Content. Get Customers*.

> As Joe shared with me, "Professional services firms can now be the leading informational expert in their niche 24 hours a day by providing the most compelling and relevant content online to their target buyers. Who knew that publishing can now be the ultimate competitive advantage for professional services firms?"

Going back to old-school Marketing 101, marketing activities are classified as either "push" or "pull" tactics. Push tactics interrupt a person and try to get them to do something. Pull tactics, in the traditional sense, are things that draw a person in, like a sale or event. Today, pull includes relationship building, conversational tactics, and becoming a trusted resource for your market.

Content marketing definitely fits best under this updated view of "pull" marketing. And one of the great things about it is that many expressions of content marketing only require your time. Unlike ad campaigns or pay-per-click marketing, it's often a very inexpensive approach for generating new leads.

Or as Joe Chernov, VP of content marketing at Eloqua, defines it in Eloqua's e-book, *Grande Guide to B2B Content Marketing*:

> "Content marketing is the art of creating, curating, and distributing valuable content, combined with the science of measuring its impact on awareness, lead generation, and customer acquisition."

Content marketing is valuable in many ways, but let's take a look at three in particular:

1. It's real.

It helps humanize your brand. Content marketing forces a company to have a content-producing mindset. When you're developing content on a regular basis, your voice is going to be heard. It's tough to put every piece of content being developed through all of the same filters that an ad might go through.

2. It's real-time.

Not all content is real-time, but live blogs, tweets, and video blogs give you an opportunity to respond to real-world events and industry news as it happens.

3. It takes real thinking.

I think if you were pressed to write down everything you knew about a particular topic in an hour, at first the task would be very intimidating. By the end of the hour, you would've probably lost track of time. The reality is, you're probably much more knowledgeable in your area of expertise than you realize. Content marketing provides an outlet to share that knowledge.

Demonstrating your depth of knowledge is something often referred to as "thought leadership."

The following two interviews reveal creative ways you can begin to use content marketing for your firm. You might also imagine how these two interviews might have worked as videos on my website or stories on my firm's blog.

"We're in a highly regulated industry. We can't do content marketing."

If you think you're in a tough spot, imagine the difficulties of getting a law firm to do content marketing. Now imagine you are in that law firm, and you're recognized as an international leader in content marketing.

Seem unlikely? Meet my new friend, AJ Huisman.

I had the pleasure of interviewing AJ awhile back and meeting him in person at the inaugural Content Marketing World conference hosted in Cleveland, OH, where he was a speaker.

AJ is the marketing director at Kennedy Van der Laan, an independent law firm based in Amsterdam. Before you assume he just walked into a firm whose culture already embraced content marketing, think again. AJ only had his firm on-board after a few months of being employed there.

Kennedy Van der Laan, like many law firms in the United States, is divided into many sections, or practice groups. Before AJ joined the firm, they had a very traditional, internally focused way of dealing with content. The challenge was to identify the proper steps to take content marketing to a higher level within the firm.

"Looking at it with more of a centralized market focus is one thing that helped," AJ says. "We took inventory of all the obvious and not so obvious content we had available. Most people don't realize they produce so much [content]; they only use it for the internal audience, to produce a newsletter for a smaller audience, or to do in-house training for just one client. Now we're using all of that content in many different ways, and sharing it with a wider audience."

AJ quickly found it wasn't just his team or the attorneys within the firm who were developing content.

"There were many people who were excited to help. For instance, we found we had a secretary on staff who was a playwright. She wanted to help tell compelling stories and jumped right in producing content for our marketing team."

AJ also has the benefit of working with a team of journalists on a contract basis, who are focused on making sure content is reusable.

"One person in particular is championing that," he notes. "That person sifts through piles of legal mumbo-jumbo to identify concepts to use for e-books, seminars, and website copy. We consider how we can frame that content within our various vertical specialties, as well as package it for our target group."

The attorneys are on-board with the initiative as well. That took some time, but through quite a few presentations and a lot of talking, he managed to get the content message across. "Most of the lawyers spend their days working on billable hours, with little time to clarify content or write anything new. That's why the content team members are connected to one or two practice areas each. They sit in on meetings, learn the lingo, and work directly with some of the junior members of the team," AJ explains.

"It was important to get the attorneys to see that with a little extra effort, their content could have much more mileage. And we also made them aware that they should focus on the core message first and elaborate from there," AJ continues. "We ask the attorneys to write out in the three sentences what they're trying to say, and to whom it is important and why."

Along those same lines, AJ says "it's important that the attorney doesn't just give us a slide deck, but also provides a short description of the main points. That's the type of thing we can send to other clients, present on a future webinar, or send to no-shows from a conference. The slide decks miss the story—they miss the voice of the presenter, so we create the story in a good-looking package."

When I spoke with AJ, he was still early in this new setup. I was curious about his next steps.

Now that his team has developed a solid process for finding and refining content within the practice groups, they're working to find out how to get on-board earlier in the process. "We need to know where the firm is trying to go and why, so it's not just 'make us a bunch of brochures.'"

It's all well and good to say you're trying to get involved earlier in the process, but how do you pull that off in practice? For Kennedy Van der Laan the most obvious way to get involved earlier was to go directly to their clients.

AJ's latest approach is to send out short and sweet questionnaires asking clients about areas of concern for their industries. If the questionnaire turns up a dissatisfied client, the firm has a chance to better respond to their needs and assess why they are not pleased.

"What we're asking is, 'What worries you? What keeps you up at night?' Then we take those answers out to the lawyers and editorial staff to create content that addresses those issues. Who cares about when we were founded or what practice groups we have? We need to provide solid answers for the business issues that our clients and prospects are struggling with."

The team also has approached a qualitative research firm that specializes in law firms to interview Kennedy Van der Laan clients.

"Sometimes it's just a matter of asking our clients, 'What is the most frustrating part of dealing with us? Is there anything bugging you?' That's part of our innovation strategy. For us, it's more than using content for marketing. We've adopted a content mindset. It's really content as conversation."

AJ has a way of making things sound so simple, even for a large, conservative organization like a law firm. And to think, English is only one of the many languages he and his team speaks!

Developing content that runs circles around your competition.

Lori Nash Byron is a brilliant marketing consultant who works with software companies and other professional services firms. I had the pleasure of hearing her present a case study while she was employed as marketing director of Orchard, Hiltz & McCliment, Inc. (OHM), a Detroit-based engineering firm. (Through acquisitions, OHM is now an engineering, architecture, and planning firm.) The case study focused on how she was able to create buzz for her employer, using educational content as a cornerstone of the approach.

As Lori recounted to me again recently, "It goes back to OHM's 'positioning' of working in the public sector only."

OHM started off in Michigan when there was a lot of residential development. The firm worked on the behalf of the community government, which could have been seen as an adversarial relationship. But according to Lori, OHM positioned the firm as doing what was best for the community, not the developers. "This helped OHM stand out from the competition," she says.

"The problem with most engineering firms is they don't differentiate," Lori continues. "Maybe it's because they're terrified of what they're not, and/or stating a firm position in the marketplace." I couldn't agree more. Unfortunately, when you claim to be terrific at everything, it's difficult to be remembered for anything.

As we've discussed in previous chapters, engineering firms, like any other professional services firm, should take a clear stance on who they are and express that clearly through their website, their voice, and even their social media presence. This is exactly what Lori sought to do for OHM

And not surprisingly, OHM's positioning did appeal to their audience. "It meant a great deal to the community that OHM was involved in local charities and the school system. Practicing what we talked about, and having a position in the marketplace that was distinctly different from our competitors was helpful, and that drove what happened online."

OHM's website positioned the firm as: "Expert advisors—in it for the long term, not just a single project. We have the experts who can guide you through the process." This drove the language, social media, and content publishing strategy.

This positioning is what led OHM to experiment with leveraging a newer engineering concept called the "diverging diamond interchange." Lori wrote an educational white paper describing the concept and what experts had to say about it. Quotes from OHM engineers were woven in.

"We published it on the OHM website and printed copies in the company newsletter," Lori says. "Surprisingly, this bumped our Google rankings on the topic with little effort. Once we saw how successful this was, and started getting phone calls from the story, we began mentioning the diverging diamond article in other posts."

Next Lori and the OHM team held a webinar about the topic and other similar design approaches for the American Society for Civil Engineers (ASCE). "It was ASCE's best-attended webinar to date, and we repeated it twice!"

At one point, the OHM article was the number two listing on a Google search for diverging diamond interchanges, just below the Wikipedia article on the topic. OHM even had a *Kansas City Star* reporter call for quotes when the first diverging diamond interchange in the U.S. opened near the city.

"For me, it's about helping my clients figure out who their ideal client is and how to reach them via speaking engagements, publishing articles, and more. That's what content marketing means to me. I don't worry so much about social media until we know what we're going to be talking about.

"At OHM, we chose the diverging diamond topic because it fit with us and our positioning," Lori adds. "We were able to speak intelligently about it, and actually drove inbound leads from this topic alone. And the most amazing part? While I worked there, we had never actually built a diverging diamond interchange."While AJ and Lori's stories are inspirational, if you read closely, you'll find that their successes came from doing little things regularly until they became habit for both themselves and their firms.

Where to start building content marketing.

With content marketing as a mindset, it's easy to find the benefits, but tough to find the starting line. We recommend starting with a small, yet foundational content marketing strategy that is within the grasp of nearly every professional services firm: blogging.

The word "blog" comes from the original idea of a "web log" or online journal. Eventually users just started saying "blog." A blog is a kind of website that has serial content—you add to it whenever you like—and it's all kept in one place.

Most basic blogging platforms are free to use, but you may need someone a bit more technical to help you get it set up and looking the way you want. WordPress, Blogger, and Tumblr are just a few options.

If you're working with a content marketing team and are ready for a more advanced tool than one of the "free" options, consider investing in a content marketing system. Compendium is one company that offers tools such as content calendars, greater administrative controls, and ways to capture client stories.

A blog is a great place to originate content for use in other places and/or to tease deeper content that you may have in a book, PDF, or white paper. You can use the same content that appears on your blog, in e-newsletters, brochures, sales sheets, and more.

Here are three great ways blogging can work for your firm:

1. Blogging is an inexpensive way to begin to develop your content marketing muscles. Writing about what you know helps you develop your voice and deepens your own understanding on a particular topic.

2. It's social. Blogging doesn't have to be limited to people who intentionally plan to visit your blog. You can share blog posts by linking to them in your email signature and through social media, which we'll discuss in greater depth in Chapters 11 and 12. You can also enable a function that allows visitors to comment. Seek bloggers you respect, and begin commenting on their blogs as well. Chances are you'll see an uptick in traffic and comments on your own blog as a result.

3. Blogging is the "gateway" to other types of content marketing. Depending on your blogging platform, you can post photo galleries, SlideShare posts, videos, infographics, and links to other content, all from your blog. So as your blogging efforts grow, so too do your content marketing opportunities!

So get out there. Get blogging, and remember: Every touch point is an opportunity to show just how professional your brand is. Make the most of each and every opportunity—be it collateral, campaign, or content.

Homework:

☐ What marketing techniques have been most effective in helping you secure the last few engagements for your company?

☐ Create your prioritized list of collateral using the "marketing priorities" and "sales opportunities" approaches.

☐ Would your firm benefit from regular campaigns? How could they be most effective?

☐ Does your firm do any regular content marketing?

☐ What would it take to create a "content marketing mindset" within your firm?

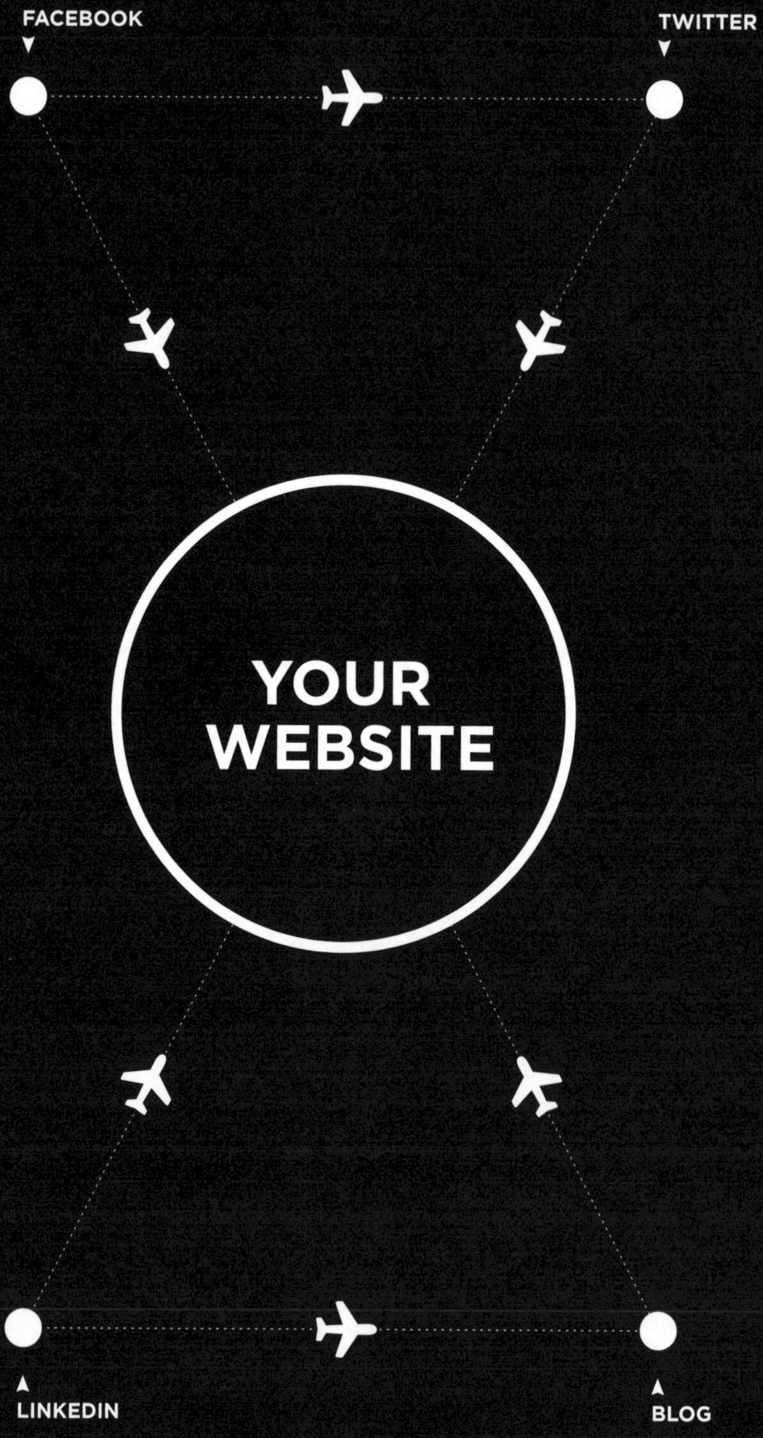
FACEBOOK
TWITTER
YOUR WEBSITE
LINKEDIN
BLOG

CHAPTER TEN

Websites & Digital Media: Identifying the Hub of Your Professional Services Brand

In business, there is no magic lever, but the Internet sure is a step in the right direction. Where should you start online, and from which site should you drive all your online communications?

> "Give me a place to stand and with a lever I will move the whole world."
>
> —Archimedes

Once you've developed your new corporate identity, the next step is to begin applying your new look and feel to your website and other online properties.

I could probably write an entire book about my firm's "branding approach" to website design—but since that's not the focus of this book, we're only going to touch on some of the high points.

Your website should be a perfect online reflection of the brand that you've worked so hard to develop. The text, images, videos, and articles should echo and reinforce the voice of your brand.

As such, your website will be an invaluable resource as a validation tool. Prospects visiting your website will quickly digest who you are, what you are about, and why they should care. And best of all, the impression they get from your website will reinforce what the marketplace has already told them about you. When prospects perceive that level of consistency, they'll experience a high level of comfort in their ability to trust your firm to solve their problems.

Your website also should be a highly efficient business development tool. It may eventually become one of your most successful sales reps. It should be not only a destination you direct prospects to, but also a tool that captures those visitors and turns them into promising leads for your business development team.

Is that how you would describe your website?

Ask yourself the following:

- Is our website starting to look a little dated?

- Does our business development team use it?

- Does the language sound like that of our nearest competitors?

- Do we know how many leads are coming from our website? If we do know, is the answer zero?

Maybe you know your website isn't cutting it. Take heart! It's not just you. This problem exists within many professional services firms. We have lovingly dubbed this the "website emergency."

Is your firm facing a website emergency?

While the redesign of your website may be the next logical step in the branding process as we've described it thus far, most clients ask us to fix their website first. In fact, we like to joke that our conference room has become a makeshift triage station for marketing patients. For the many reasons we've already discussed, websites seem to be the most common marketing emergency that our design firm encounters.

In fact, if I asked 100 professional services firms if their websites were "under the weather" or worse, I'd be willing to bet that more than two-thirds of them would say yes.

An ill-performing website (more often than not) is the symptom of a larger positioning problem, rather than the problem itself. But that doesn't change the fact that these websites are presenting some serious symptoms.

Luckily for you, if you've been following along in the book so far, you have a much tighter handle on positioning. So whether you're redesigning your website to better reflect your brand or you're building it for the first time, here are the Top 10 things we recommend avoiding. We've divided these "emergencies" into several categories.

Content emergencies.

Even from within your firm, it's often easy to spot a dated look or a button that doesn't work. Unfortunately, content problems can be tougher to locate. Here are the top content-related issues we regularly combat:

1. "It's all about us."

When was the last time you visited a site to read their mission statement? Does your site inspire visitors with compelling messages and fantastic photography? Does it offer them what they're looking for, or does it focus on your firm's history and go on and on about your mission?

Think about why you take the time to read another company's website. When was the last time you surfed around wanting to read mission statements? I mean, really.

Which pages are most important from a content standpoint? From our vantage point, the most regularly visited pages on a professional services website are the homepage, about us, contact, and bio pages. Blogs and case studies aren't always the most visited pages, but visitors to these pages tend to stay longer.

2. Ignoring the value.

Most professional services businesses are highly relationship-driven. Not just online relationships, but real, human relationships. That's a great thing, but it's not an excuse to have a dated, less than professional website. Your present clients may excuse your sub-par site, but they're not your only potential visitors.

Your website's number one opportunity is to serve as a validation tool for new prospects and future employees of your firm. These visitors don't have the benefit of an existing relationship with you. Your website may be the first impression they develop of your firm.

3. Poor-quality content and photography.

If your photos and website copy don't hold your attention, they surely won't impress anyone else. Spend some quality time on what you're saying, and only show off your best work.

I once had a piece in my student design portfolio of a billboard for a steakhouse. It wasn't my best work, but it was a real-life billboard. I was fortunate enough to have a professional advise me, "Who cares if it's a real billboard? If it's not your best work, don't keep it in your portfolio."

I think it's good to adopt this same philosophy about your website. If the photos and other pieces of content aren't showing your firm at its best, get rid of them.

4. Static content.

Some static content is okay, but you should strive to give visitors a reason to come back. Search engines love fresh content, too. Does your site still say ©2007 or worse? Yikes. One great fix to this problem is to build your website on a platform or content management system that allows you to make simple text, photo, and other content updates on the fly, as-needed.

Ideally, you should be updating your content on a regular basis. But perhaps things at your firm don't change very often. What should you update in that instance? Consider scheduling regular updates for your website once per quarter. Think about updating news stories, your client list, or just reviewing your service offerings. Have you added anything new? Is there anything that should be removed? Chances are you can make updates at least a few times per year.

5. One-way communication.

Are you providing avenues for feedback or conversation? What's your call-to-action? Blogs, videos, and social media are great tactics to consider.

Do whatever makes sense for your firm, but don't limit the conversation on your website to what you're saying in the text.

Design emergencies.

Obviously the design of your site should be in-line with your new corporate identity standards, taking full advantage of your unique positioning, voice, and look. However, here are a few items to be aware of:

6. Too much Flash.

Remember all of those sites that used to have long intro animations? How many times did you click "skip intro?"

It's impossible to know exactly where technology will go next, but Adobe has abandoned further mobile development for Flash.

If Flash intros are dead, having an entirely Flash-based site or Flash navigation may be far worse. If prospects try to view your Flash site on an iPhone or iPad, the site may be partially or completely invisible. Plus, if your site is completely Flash-based, it may not be as indexable by Google and other search engines.

The good news is that today, languages such as JavaScript or HTML5 are being used to achieve site-wide motion that is viewable on iOS devices and recognizable by search engines. I'm not saying you can't have motion or video on your website, just be sure that your method of delivering moving content doesn't distract the user or prevent the content from being viewed on popular devices.

7. Your visitors are lost.

What do you want your visitors to do when they arrive on your homepage? Get inspired? Contact you? Visit your blog? Sign up for your newsletter? Many websites fall short when it comes to a call-to-action or moving visitors through the site. Make sure that what you want the visitor to do is clear.

8. Avant-garde navigation.

Remember the first website you saw with navigation that floated around the screen? As your mouse chased the buttons, graphic elements darted across your monitor. It was cool…until you couldn't find what you were looking for, right?

If visitors can't find their way around your website, your navigation may be a little too clever. Your navigation isn't a place to try something wacky on your website. Keep it simple and don't make visitors work too hard.

SEO emergencies.

SEO is the practice of helping a website rank higher for a particular search term. The following are very basic optimization tips, but still a good place to start if you're new to SEO:

9. Invisible to search engines.

Google your company or your service category and market (e.g., Indianapolis Architects). Did you find your firm on the first page? No? Well neither did your potential client.

A very small percentage of searchers today go to the second

page of search results. And after the third page of results, almost all searchers drop off.

If you have a generic company name, or an entirely Flash-based site, these are contributing to the problem. In addition, consider how regularly you're updating your site content, blog, or posting to social media or social bookmarking sites.

It's good to understand what your website is and is not being found for. You may have great success with some terms, and less with others. We'll talk more about what your website should be found under at the end of this chapter.

10. No measurements.

How many visitors does your site average each month? What's the most popular content on your site? What search terms do visitors use to locate your website? How do visitors find you? If you're not checking your stats, you'll never know.

Most hosting companies provide free access to these statistics. If yours doesn't, spend a few minutes adding Google Analytics or a similar stats package to your site. Many of them are free and they'll provide you with data on traffic, visitors, lengths of visits, and much more.

Make an effort to review web analytics at least once a month to determine if your activity over the past month has actually yielded any results.

And last but not least, the website leadership emergency.

Sometimes the biggest challenge is deciding who will take ownership of the website from a marketing perspective. That person will need to make ongoing decisions about how often to make updates, how to drive more traffic, and how to convert that traffic to qualified leads.

Sometimes this role is filled by an employee of the company, and other times it's an outside consultant. But either way, the website needs a leader.

I have a hunch that if you're reading this book, the best person for this job is probably you. Congratulations!

Eliminate website emergencies: How to go from bad to bold.

So how do we overcome these challenges? How can your firm develop a web presence that is consistent with your new brand strategy and also drives leads?

To drive leads, we first must drive engagement. Engagement goes beyond mere "visits." Engagement means that your visitors are interacting with your site, reading content, requesting information, sharing your site with friends, or coming back regularly. Engaged visitors are potential prospects, future employees, and sometimes just peers from your industry.

What does it take to get visitors engaged with your brand online?

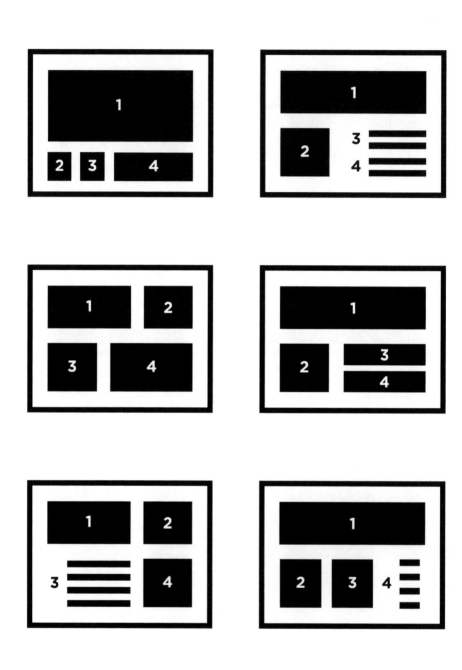

The four levels of online brand engagement.

1. Be found.

If a website wins an award in the forest and no one is there to click on it, does it still generate leads?

Please excuse the silly example, but consider this very real problem. If you have the best website in the country, and yet no one visits the site or knows how to get there, it's not very effective.

There are several reasons why websites fail to be found. Perhaps the architecture of the site makes it difficult for it to be identified by search engines. Or maybe the site isn't being marketed very well, if at all. But the bottom line is, being found is the very first level of engagement for your brand online.

2. Pass the two-second test.

In my very unscientific research, I've found that most websites are allowed about two seconds to demonstrate that they're the site the searcher was looking for.

Don't believe me? Think about the last time you searched for something you knew little about. You entered the search phrase. Hit go. Scanned the list. Clicked on the first item...and I would argue that within the first two seconds of viewing that site, you made the decision to either dig deeper, or hit the back button to further your search.

When a website passes the two-second test, it usually has one or more of the following qualities: captivating headlines, images, or design; obvious placement of keywords, products, or brand names; or an easily recognizable, branded look.

When a visitor finds your site, does it pass his or her two-second test? The surest way to determine that is to review your website analytics. Pay particular attention to the "time on page" and "bounce rate," which can both be indicative of search behavior.

3. Invite users to dig deeper.

Okay, let's say your site passes the two-second test. Now what?

Your site should provide enough valuable information to encourage the visitor to dig deeper into your site. Whether your point-of-view is something every visitor will agree with, or your philosophy rings true isn't the point. Not everyone will be your client. But does your site at least get them deep enough that they can begin to qualify themselves?

How do you measure this? Again, take a look at your website analytics. Consider the "number of pages per visit" and "average time on site."

4. Drive visitors to take action.

I have a few friends who always meet in coffee shops, and yet, they themselves don't drink coffee. Comfy chairs, convenient locations, free Wi-Fi. These are all great reasons to visit your local coffee shop. However, I'm fairly confident that those coffee shop owners didn't set up shop for their neighbors to just hang out with them. Their goal is to sell coffee.

Sometimes websites end up doing something similar. These sites may draw thousands of visits per month, and yet yield no immediate action.

So once your site is found, passes the two-second test, and encourages visitors to dig deeper, the final goal is to create action.

What is your call-to-action? And better yet, what constitutes action online? For every business it's probably a little different, but here are some of the most common types of action: fill out a contact form, make a phone call, subscribe to an e-newsletter, or download a white paper or other document. And beyond the more "traditional" online calls-to-action are a new breed of social calls-to-action. These include "liking" something, becoming a fan, friending, subscribing to a blog or podcast, tweeting, forwarding to a friend, and other types of social sharing.

First things first.

What is the most important thing that you hope your visitors see, read, or do while visiting your homepage?

I think one of the most overlooked consideRations in redesigning a website is determining what you want visitors to do once they arrive. Your website may be like the dog that caught the car. Your visitors are here, but now what?

Or perhaps the main thing you want your visitors to do IS on your homepage. But is it obvious? Here's a hint. If everything is bold, italic, caps, red, or big on your page, everything is fighting for prominence on the page. If everything looks important, nothing will actually stand out on its own.

How do you get the important details to stand out from the rest?

To begin, think about the hierarchy of each element on your homepage. Make a list of the five most important elements on your page. Perhaps it looks something like this:

1. Who are we? Logo, name, etc.

2. What do we do? We specialize in a particular service.

3. Call-to-action. Click here to see our latest and greatest project.

4. Contact info. How to reach us.

5. Navigation. Here's how to explore further.

Your list may be longer than five items, and certainly may be in a different order, but try this exercise first to determine what's most important on the page. Next, think about the less important elements that also belong on the homepage. Last, cut any elements that are not necessary to have on the page at all. If possible, do this for every page.

Next, express this list of hierarchy visually. We call these wireframes. It's a simple activity you can do on a whiteboard. Draw boxes that represent each element on the page. Which is most important visually? Is that reflected both in your ordered list and your wireframe? Great! Now you can use these wireframes to design a more successful website.

In the end, the importance of each element should translate to the visual hierarchy of the finished website design. And of course, test out different theories. If you think a red button may drive more clicks than the old blue button, test it out and see if your theory holds true. Unlike a brochure, a website never "goes to print" so you can make infinite tweaks, seeking to constantly improve the overall user experience.

But your website is just one of many online tactics you'll likely consider. There are blogs, social media, email marketing, landing pages, and more.

Which online tactics should you explore first?

Of course your website isn't the only online presence you need to keep in mind. In fact, it's easy to be overwhelmed by all of the online tools that professional services businesses can choose from. So how do you determine and prioritize which tactics to pursue and which to ignore?

Well—what's your strategy? We had a client this past year wonder aloud if their Facebook fans should select their next logo. To me, that was a scary proposition. Unless your strategy is "leave everything to chance," having your fans determine major business decisions is the opposite of following a business strategy.

It's not any different when it comes to determining which online media to pursue. Your strategy should drive your decisions.

Is your strategy to be top-of-mind with your friends and family, health care companies across the country, or with 12 specific CEOs who run businesses within your county? Your answers to these types of questions will help you determine if it makes sense to have an engaging Facebook page, or to spend more time getting cited at websites that report on local business news.

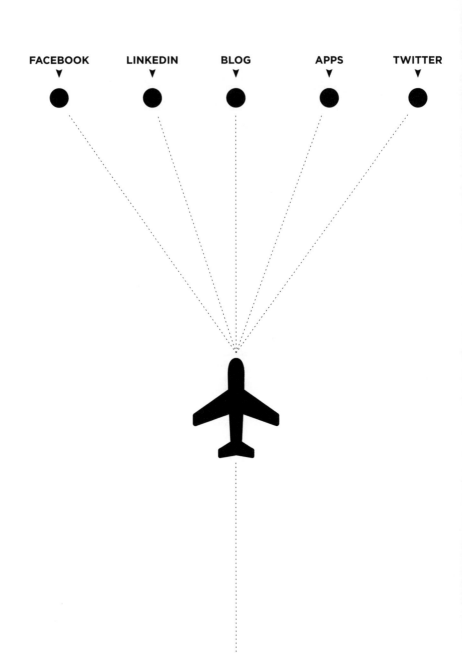

What is your hub?

As with an airline, having one primary location to run traffic to and from helps simplify your ability to do business online. Identifying your online hub is a major step toward carving out your online brand strategy. Here's an example:

Let's say you decide to elevate your company website as the hub of your brand. In short, that means that the goal of subsequent actions online should drive visitors back to your website. Whether you are sending out an email marketing message, sponsoring a display ad, or tweeting or posting to your Facebook page—you should always drive visitors back to your website.

Of course, every message shouldn't just overtly scream CLICK HERE! But as a rule, think about driving traffic back to your online hub.

Another benefit of identifying your hub is that it will help you determine what other online tools you'd like to have and when they should be developed. If you sit today with a dated website, no blog, no apps, and no social networks, don't despair. If you're confused about where your hub is supposed to be, go back to your strategy document. Once you're able to develop and maintain your hub at a respectable level, you can move on to additional tactics that will expand your reach.

If you want to grow your online presence, keep this in mind: If you don't have time to make each endeavor as high-quality as you and your visitors expect it to be, you're not ready to develop it. Whether it's a blog, a Facebook page, or simply getting started on Twitter, do each to the best of your ability, or wait until you're fully ready to start working on them.

RatioArchitects.com

Our company was hired in 2009 by Ratio Architects, an award-winning design and planning firm, to redesign their entire web presence.

The previous Ratio website had several technical issues that were hindering the firm from using the site as a primary means for attracting new business. First, the site was built entirely in Flash, so it was impossible for Ratio to make quick, timely updates themselves or post recent project news. As a result of the Flash-based site, their website content was essentially invisible to search engines like Google and Yahoo. On top of that, the site had no analytics package, so the Ratio team couldn't really see how the site was performing.

And their signature projects were difficult for visitors to locate—a real problem for a high-end architectural firm with a portfolio of impressive work.

Ratio was among the first large architecture firms that we worked with. As part of the redesign, we also built their blog. Ratio was new to blogging, but the framework that we created, along with their commitment to regularly publishing original content, created what I would call a "culture of competition," making the Ratio website a fantastic hub of thought leadership content.

From a quasi-outsider's perspective, I think having multiple employees contribute to their blog helped push each of them to create more and even better content. To me, this seemed like a very positive outcome.

And the content wasn't limited to the blog. Long after our initial work on the website and blog was complete, Ratio remained committed to producing new, ongoing content. We later incorporated capabilities to better feature video, social media, and more throughout the website.

In 2010, the Society for Marketing Professional Services (SMPS) awarded RatioArchitects.com the best professional services website in the country. The SMPS judges noted that the inclusion of video, social media, blogging, and other content was what helped differentiate Ratio's site from the 35 national and international entries..

Of course, design competitions are often seen as simply beauty competitions. Not that there's anything wrong with having a pretty website, but in Ratio's case, this site had some serious performance metrics as well.

"Three months after the new site launch, Google Analytics showed that our site traffic increased by 68 percent with 67.36 being unique visits," says Tony Steinhardt, FSMPS, CPSM, principal of the firm.

"The numbers also showed that visitors viewed an average of 4.41 pages per visit; that the average bounce rate was 30.32 percent; and that visitors spent an average time of three minutes and 24 seconds on the site – two times the industry average of one minute, thirty seconds," he continues.

A website with beauty, and brains? Now that's something any architecture firm would be excited about!

How SEO can help your positioning.

Another important consideRation is how your firm ranks with search engines. According to a white paper originally published by Enquiro (now part of Mediative, a Yellow Pages Group company), more than 70 percent of B2B purchasers report using a search engine at the start of their buying process. If you're not visible during these searches, you're going to miss out on getting in on early purchasing discussions.

Also consider this: If your firm is highly specialized, wouldn't it be natural for it to come up in a search for that specialty?

Take a few minutes to brainstorm a few potential search phrases that you'd like to be found under. Think about how you would word these phrases and how prospects might word them differently. For example, you might say "sustainable architects Indianapolis" and your prospect might type "who is the best green architect in Indy?"

After you document these terms, input them into your favorite search engine. Who comes up on the first and second page for each? Are you anywhere to be found? What does this tell you?

Imagine all of your hard work to differentiate and position your professional services brand, only to have it fail at SEO. Good SEO should harmonize your branding, positioning, and web design.

If it's not something your firm is paying attention to yet, it's time to take a look.

Beyond search.

Of course, there are many ways to drive traffic to your website outside of search. You can market your URL using traditional off-line methods, include links in your email signatures, and promote your website via social media. I realize that just the thought of exploring social media is scary to many of you, and we'll address those fears in the next two chapters. For now, begin to explore all the potential you have for getting your website in front of the right prospects.

Homework:

☐ Where does your current website fall short?

☐ Does your website pass the two-second test?

☐ Are visitors engaged enough to want
to return?

☐ What is the hub of your brand online? What
should it be?

☐ How does your website stack up in search?

negativity

greatness

polarization

Fear of...

change

commitment

CHAPTER ELEVEN

The Five Fears of Social Media

Should your professional services firm participate in social media? What if it's just a passing fad?

> "So, first of all, let me assert my firm belief that the only thing we have to fear is fear itself."
>
> —Franklin D. Roosevelt

F_____.

Fear.

It's the ultimate four-letter word.

It holds so many of us back from finding our greatness.

Why is that?

Last year, I had the honor of speaking at the 2011 Society of Marketing Professional Services Conference in Sacramento. While there, I sat in on a social media panel discussion. For about an hour, leaders from some of the top engineering and architectural firms in the world shared their experiences, challenges, and successes in social media. And while about half of the panel members had some very cutting-edge approaches (especially for large companies), the other half seemed to have barely dipped their toes.

Even more disconcerting were some of the questions raised by the audience. They all seemed to hint at an underlying concern: "is social media a good thing for us to pursue?"

We Midwesterners often joke that we're not always the first movers. In fact, I've heard plenty of fears voiced when it comes to social media. But what I learned in California was that these fears are quite common nationwide.

But really, folks—there's nothing to fear. The firms that are seeing impressive results from their social media efforts will tell you just that.

If you're suffering from analysis paralysis when it comes to social media, know this: if you continue to stay on the sidelines, your opportunity to stay top-of-mind with your market may fade. Each day that you avoid social media is another day that your competition can build momentum online.

Intimidated by technology.

I'm often told that professionals don't get into social media because they're somewhat intimidated by the technology.

Let me tell you a story about a financial planner I know. I'm pretty familiar with this story, because this guy is my dad.

I wanted to share this story for two reasons. One, I think it's a good parallel example to these social media fears; and two, it's a good litmus test to see if my parents are reading this book!

My dad is in his early 60s. Most of his business is done either in person, across the table, or over the phone. He actually just joined the "cell phone" generation about 10 years ago. He's still using very little of what his phone can do—outside of checking golf scores, reviewing the financial markets, and making calls.

One feature in particular that he ignored for quite some time was voice mail. Only a select few of his clients have his mobile number, so he always figured they would leave a message at his office or email him.

My dad would probably tell you that he didn't check his voice mail because he didn't have to. There's probably some truth to that, but deep down inside, I think he felt it was a hassle to figure out how to listen to his messages. Maybe he was a little scared of the technology—especially at first.

Now to be fair, my dad has always had a Blackberry. I'm not sure I'd know how to check the voicemail on a Blackberry either. I'm an Apple snob.

Nevertheless, my dad just told me that with his newest phone he is finally checking voice mail.

So my dad is finally checking his voicemail, and about that same time, my mom informs me she's following me on Twitter! Imagine my surprise. *Note to self: no more making fun of my parents on Twitter.*

Held back by resistance.

Speaking of resistance to new technologies, I'm well aware that many professionals aren't big on chasing after the latest and greatest. However, I'm still surprised when I see studies that document the level of their resistance.

Jeremy Victor, founder of Make Good Media and editor of B2Bbloggers.com, wrote a blog post in August 2011 about the Top 20 most socially active B2B industries. Guess what? Architecture, Engineering, Construction, Legal, and Accounting were nowhere to be found.

Why is that? Perhaps your firm doesn't "see the payoff," or is just "naturally resistant" to new things, but I think it all boils down to fear.

Of course, we could talk about social media fears in a very tactical sense—being afraid to blog, or nervous about tweeting. But I'm suggesting these fears are rooted in deeper, more common fears we share as humans. How can professional services providers get beyond these fears?

Let's start by taking a closer look at what I call the five fears of social media.

Fear of negativity.

Let me state this plain and simple: Negativity is unavoidable. People will say negative things about your brand, your company, and your people, regardless of your level of participation in the conversation.

The truth is, it's probably already happening. I'm not trying to make you paranoid, but it's foolish to think that there haven't already been nasty, negative things said about you in emails, conversations, and perhaps even in blogs, videos, tweets, Facebook posts, etc.

So if it's already going on, should you just hide your head in the sand? Maybe if you just avoid the conversation, do you think it will blow over?

How do you combat negativity?

The remedy for the fear of negativity is to accept that there are people in this world who will always want to complain or say bad things, regardless of how great your firm is.

Negative conversations are unregulated and unbelievably powerful. If you opt not to join the discussion online, it's not going to get any better. Denial does not stop the conversation.

Okay, you might say, but social media is so bleeding edge that nobody else is really "out there" talking about professional businesses, right? Wrong.

The social media conversation grows at an exponential rate:

• Facebook has more than 845 million users

• Twitter has more than 200 million users

• LinkedIn has 150 million users

• And the newest act in town, Google+, has 90 million users and counting...

If you accept that even the smallest fractions of these users might be your clients, there's certainly cause for concern. The conversation has been going on without you. So what can you do?

Do what marketers do best, and start telling your story. Join in. And try to do more than just tell us what you had for breakfast. Make it interesting and just be yourself. I think you'll find there's less fear of negativity when you're actually part of the conversation.

And perhaps just as important, if negative things are being said about your brand on social media, the ability to respond in real-time to these comments is invaluable. Quickly and professionally addressing negative comments may actually turn negative incidents into positive outcomes.

Fear of polarization.

The second common fear may be a bit more hidden and harder to recognize. Maybe it sounds something like this:

> "Please accept my resignation. I don't want to belong to any club that will accept people like me as a member."

> -Groucho Marx, from a telegram to the now-defunct Friars Club of Beverly Hills, to which he once belonged, as recounted in his book *Groucho and Me*

Some of us think that if people get to know too much about us, our brand, or our business—if they get to know the "real" us—they may no longer want to do business with us.

This fear may drive you to present yourself as someone you are not. Perhaps you withhold your opinion or point-of-view. Perhaps you're just trying to blend in. Maybe you have the right intentions, but you think people will see you as a fake.

A true challenge with the fear of polarization is that you have to accept that not everybody will like you. And in my estimation, you don't want everyone to like you. Your flavor of "like" should polarize. Perhaps some will love you, and in that thin line between love and hate you will know that some will dislike you.

As one of my favorite teachers often said, "Don't straddle the barbed wire fence. Pick a side."

Religion, politics, and money. Ready to tip over some sacred cows? Where you draw the line over what you discuss online is up to you. I was talking with a friend of mine about this recently. He joked that his "Twitter self" was a bit of a persona.

"So it's not you?" I asked.

"No, it's me. Just not ALL of me. There are just some topics I'm not going to talk about online," he said.

"I like to think of that as more of a 'sliver' than a 'persona'—it just sounds more transparent," I replied.

My feeling is that you have to pick what you do and don't want to discuss over social media. Talking or not talking about controversial topics is up to you. But for Pete's sake, say something different. Have a point-of-view. An opinion. Let us see how you think differently.

Social media can feel a bit like a popularity contest, but it's one of sworn allegiance rather than mild association. If you want your social media followers to be passionate about you, your firm, or your brand, you have to be different. Pick a side of the barbed wire fence. Don't be afraid to be polarizing.

How do you get through the fear of polarization? You must first understand that people buy what they love—not what they just like. A small group of people who swear by your brand is a lot better than a larger group of people who just tolerate you. The most important thing to do for these loyal followers is recognize and reward them.

negative **SAFE?** positive

I understand why some people think that blending in is the safe move. Staying right in the middle doesn't create any enemies. But it doesn't create any raving fans either.

Think about the top stories in the NFL. Who makes the headlines? Who sells the most jerseys? The utility players who give a B+ effort every week? The backup quarterbacks who hold the clipboards? No, it's the standouts. Sometimes they're the superstars, and sometimes they're the ones getting arrested, but all of them play outside the bounds of "safe," and that's what gets the media's attention.

Let's look at this differently. What do you think your prospects are looking for when they include you in an RFP? I'd suggest if they're looking at 10 boring, similar options, they're trying to find the one firm that isn't going to blow it. When they're all the same, the prospect will probably go with the boring, safe option. But what if one of the options was different? What if that firm had a personality, a point-of-view, and a bit of swagger? Do you think that could tip the scales?

Are you boring on social media? I'm probably guilty of it sometimes. I typically talk about design, branding, business, professional services, or other B2B marketing topics. Lately, I've been trying to share more of my personal experiences. One way I like to do that is to post to my social networks via Instagram, a photo sharing app on my iPhone.

One such post was of the wakeboarding competition happening in our office park this summer. A former client of ours responded to my tweet, noting that my office "just got 10,000 times cooler."

A week later, that client handed us a new branding project. Did my tweet earn us a project? No, our capabilities and past performance earned the project. The tweet just kept us top-of-mind with our former client. Sometimes cutting through the clutter and sharing what's happening around you is enough to be memorable.

I think architectural publishing mogul Mark Zweig says it best: "It's time to shake it up!"

Do you think staying in the safe and boring middle counts as "shaking it up?" Be polarizing!

Fear of commitment.

This fear first expresses itself as a fear of committing to a focus within your firm. I think the most obvious example is the all-too-common, "we do a little bit of everything" positioning.

First of all, "everything" isn't memorable. It can't be. Second, you're not taking a position that anyone can get excited about. You're straddling the barbed wire fence. You have to assume a stance.

The fear of committing to a focus also expresses as a fear of committing to social media marketing because it appears to be a "giant waste of time."

Sure there are wasteful ways to spend time on social media. Like any other productive marketing activity, it requires having a strategy. Your team needs to remember there's a difference between social networking and social NOTworking.

But what if you already have a good sales and marketing strategy? What if you commit time to social media and don't get any response? Aren't there better uses of your time? Why should you divide your focus and engage in this new media?

Why indeed.

According to HubSpot, 69 percent of B2B marketers planned to shift their budget toward social media in 2011. Social media was the top shift, followed by virtual events and SEO.

Social media, of course, is not a silver bullet for your marketing plan. However, there's no denying that traditional intrusion marketing is dying and will soon be a thing of the past (intrusion being the act of sending unsolicited messages to an end user and expecting them to respond).

Unsolicited direct mail, untargeted email blasts, and mass telemarketing are quickly being replaced with education and entertainment strategies such as blogging, white papers, webinars, "Lunch and Learns," and other types of continuing education. Why? One very specific reason: People are protecting their time like never before because they seem to have less and less of it, while being asked to produce more and more. An intrusion of any kind will quickly be looked at as outright criminal and if you aren't leveraging "permission strategies," you may find yourself in the way of the dinosaur.

If you're feeling fearful about focusing, take a look back at your positioning strategy:

Who are we? What do we do? Who are we not?

Which social networks should you pursue? Should you concentrate on more than one? Should you just do a little bit of everything, or focus?

Have you ever heard something like this?

"I don't think our customer is on social media, especially not Twitter."

I think the challenge is to find out. How do you know where your clients spend their time online? Here's a wild idea: ask. That's right, send out a survey. Or call them. Any excuse to demonstrate that you're paying attention to your clients and want to know what they think is a great reason to touch base.

You may be surprised at what you find.

In years past, just finding a way to easily survey clients and collect the data may have seemed complicated and expensive, but with the rise of affordable (and sometimes free) email surveying tools such as SurveyMonkey, MailChimp, and the like, those excuses of the past are thrown out the window.

I think the biggest mistake that professional services firms make was something I heard echoed in Sacramento:

Don't confuse your individual client with his or her employer organization.

In professional services, some of our clients are large, traditional, slow-moving organizations. The state government. Institutions of higher education. Health care organizations. However, it's a mistake to assume that all of the key decision-makers who work for these institutions are as slow to adopt new things as their employers.

Your client is a person. Some of them may be more fearful of social media than you are, but it doesn't hurt to ask. And while you're at it, don't just ask if they're active online, but find out where they spend their time, and why.

CPI Took the Social Media Leap

My friend Chris Dellen runs a business called Communications Products, Inc. (CPI), that sells VoIP phone systems. He regularly posts YouTube videos at his blog to help tell simple stories about complex products.

He's not the biggest. CPI doesn't manufacture any of the products they sell. However, the educationally focused technology stories Chris shares on his blog provide answers to the questions his prospects are asking. And what's more, CPI's blog isn't just answering questions, it's creating conversations and building a community of clients, users, prospects, and technical experts.

> "Prospects tell us we answer more of their questions on our blog than their current vendor," Chris says. "Anybody who says they can't generate leads through social media is smoking something."

Chris' stories help him close deals. It's not hocus-pocus—he just decided to share his point-of-view, focused on creating a blog with video, and jumped in to tell his story.

As Chris' example shows, it pays to put your fears aside and to embrace this completely new type of marketing. Social media marketing strategies are very powerful, and when executed properly, will have a positive impact on your business.

The way to get over the fear of commitment is to understand the potential of new relationships with your customers. Social media can fundamentally change how they see you—not just as a vendor, but as a friend, educator, and even a business partner. Your relationship can change from being an intrusive marketer to a welcome and respected advisor.

Fear of change.

The next fear is perhaps the greatest for many. It is the fear of change.

The fear of change is very common. Many people fear change simply because change yielded pain in the past.

I see the fear of change all the time. Most of my new clients arrive knowing they need to change, but are deathly afraid to pull the trigger on their own.

A prospective client came into my office last month and boldly shared he was ready to do something different. It was time to "update their materials."

He knew he needed something new, but he was scared to death. He didn't tell me he was scared, but I could sense it. Sure, he was confident about his professional abilities—he had built a $30 million dollar business. But he couldn't figure out how to grow it from there.

The truth is, the things that helped him grow his business to $30 million were not going to be the same things that would help him grow to $50 million or $100 million.

Here's the bottom line:

What got you here isn't going to get you there!

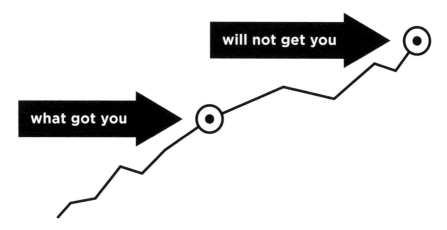

Our prospect knew something needed to change, but the idea of completely rethinking his marketing approach was frightening. In fact, as it turns out, too frightening for him to green light.

Maybe you're stuck between a rock and a hard place. You're on board with social media, but the firm leadership as a whole is reluctant to change. How can you get them off of the starting line?

In the book *Switch: How to Change Things When Change is Hard*, authors Chip Heath and Dan Heath give one of the best explanations I've heard of how to get people past the fear of change. They break down our conscience into two parts: the "elephant" (emotion) and the "rider" (logic).

The Heaths basically argue that if the elephant (emotion) is free to run wild, there isn't much the rider (logic) can do to steer or stop in. On the contrary, if you can get both emotion and logic to work together (i.e., get the rider to steer the elephant), change can happen.

Interestingly enough, my brother, friend, and pastor (yes, all the same guy) Lucas Miles shares a similar concept. Pastor Lucas finds that as people are exposed to new concepts and are emotionally charged, their first reaction is to learn everything they can about the concept.

Think about the last new idea or pastime you felt excited about. What was the first thing you did once you got into it? You probably looked for others who also were passionate about the topic, searched for books, and even more likely, researched the topic online. Your passion for the new concept fueled your hunger for more information. And in turn, your newfound knowledge about the topic excited you, creating even more positive emotions.

However, Pastor Lucas also cautions, "When you fail to find enough information to back up your emotion, the emotions begin to fade."

Your team's interest in social media may also fade if you fail to keep them both inspired and informed. So as you get them all fired-up about using social media marketing, don't forget to provide ample information to keep them rooted in both emotion and information. Ideally, an ongoing social media strategy accompanied by regular reporting should satisfy both ends of the spectrum.

Fear of greatness.

Finally, there is the fear of greatness. This may be the toughest fear you face as a marketer looking to leverage social media, or any other new marketing strategy for that matter.

The fear of being great is usually tied to two fundamental questions: Are we good enough to stand in the spotlight? Do we deserve to be recognized as leaders in our field? The fear of being great is tied to your organization's sense of self worth and your firm's confidence in its collective intellectual property.

Do you have the stuff to stand in the spotlight?

The short answer is, your firm is probably a lot smarter collectively than it gives itself credit for.

In his book *Outliers*, Malcolm Gladwell suggests that anybody who has 10,000 hours in a discipline is a comparative expert in that discipline. If you started adding up the hours of time your people have been working within their area of expertise, you might be surprised by how deep your firm's expertise actually runs. The countless hours you have been doing what you do make you incredibly valuable to others.

Sharing your expertise is not narcissistic. People are looking for experts, so don't be afraid to share what you know.

One little caveat: Social media isn't the place to scream, "I'm an EXPERT!" Be humble and sooner or later the good work that you do will shine through. You will connect with clients, convert them into fans, and they will help you carry the flag. You will attract new prospects from around the globe, just by sharing your experience and your point of view.

So, make a commitment to share your expertise and get your firm ready for the spotlight!

Getting past the fears.

Here are a few practical tips for pushing through each of the fears.

Negativity.

Do you actually have negative press online? The only thing that can dominate negative content is more content. Your best bet is to start writing. In this case, your goal should be to get some positive stories into the marketplace to demonstrate that the negative stories are the exception, not the rule. Consider some of these tactics:

- Release case studies of high-profile clients.

- Show a before-and-after.

- Highlight a client testimonial or video testimonial.

- Start a blog.

Polarization.

Are you afraid of being polarizing?

- Understand that "like" can be lethal.

- Love is a virtue. What brands do you love? Are they "safe"?

- Recognize and reward your core audience—make your fans and followers feel loved in return.

- Make it easy for your clients to engage again and again.

Commitment.

Are you worried that social media may be pulling too much attention away from other tasks? Remember, there's a difference between social networking and social NOTworking.

- Track your time on social media. See where you're getting the best return.

- Use one network to feed others. I user Twitter to feed my LinkedIn profile.

- Consider a social media aggregator (e.g., TweetDeck, HootSuite, CoTweet), so you can monitor multiple networks from one dashboard.

Change.

Are you anything but a change junkie? Think about how you can:

- Cultivate emotion and inspiration—what is the most alluring element of social media? Make yourself a picture or chart to envision it daily.

- Follow the data—what metrics are most important for you to hit? Check them weekly.

- Plan it out—create an actionable, complete plan with numbers, dates, and pictures.

Greatness.

There's a fine line between humble and foolish. If you're still having difficulty standing up and saying something on social media:

- Count up your firm's collective experience in hours.

- Print out that number in huge type on a piece of paper.

- Take it to your next marketing meeting.

- Commit to sharing your firm's collective expertise.

I'll leave you with this: Think of every other fear you've conquered. What was it? The fear of heights? Darkness? Being alone? For me, it was swimming. I'm still not an awesome swimmer, but in the end there was only one thing that helped me begin to relax in the water: I had to get in. And you can do the same. You just have to jump in and try it out.

Homework:

☐ Is your firm scared of social media?
Why or why not?

☐ Which fear is most prevalent within your
firm: Negativity, Polarization, Commitment,
Change, or Greatness?

☐ How can you help demonstrate the benefits
of using social media marketing to your firm?

☐ How will you demonstrate your progress?

CHAPTER TWELVE

Beyond the Fears: Social Media Basics

And then it hits you. "We really should be using social media to market our firm...but where do we start?"

> "All the little birdies on Jaybird Street love to hear the robin go tweet tweet tweet."
>
> —Jimmie Thomas, songwriter

If you helped your firm grow past its fears of social media, first of all, congratulations!

Second of all, it's time to start mapping out how exactly you plan to use social media to market your firm.

Popular social networks seem to pop up out of nowhere. What, you're not using Flabbler yet? It's the greatest! While we can't cover everything in this chapter that will happen in social media in the future, we can get you started with a strategy.

Social media will always be in flux.

It's important to get over the feeling that you need to control social media. You will probably never feel 100 percent caught up on your various social networks. There will always be more you could do. And there will always be a new medium to explore.

So should you just give up? Not at all! You'll just have to decide as a firm which networks are most important for your efforts, and which activities are most worth your time.

Go back to your brand strategy.

Your brand strategy will help you determine where your time will be well spent online. After reviewing your brand brief, what are your gut feelings about where you should commit your resources?

Most of all, think about why you want to be active on social media. Are you recruiting? Do you need new leads? Are you online to talk to your clients? Think about it.

A great place to begin: LinkedIn.

If you are not yet set up on LinkedIn, it's a great place to begin.

This network is one of the more "mainstream" social networks for business professionals, and it has a positive reputation across many industries. Chances are, the decision makers who work for your clients are already on LinkedIn.

LinkedIn enables you to connect with many other business professionals. Some of these connections will be people you already know, and others may be people you want to know. Making connections on LinkedIn is very similar to real-life networking. If you don't know someone, introduce yourself or ask someone else to introduce you.

How many connections should you have? It's up to you. Adding more connections doesn't win you any prizes, but Google is rumored to pay more attention to user profiles with 500 or more connections. That's not a reason to connect with just anyone, but it's worth noting.

In addition to making connections, LinkedIn is quickly replacing the need for having a professional resume. Many professionals use LinkedIn to demonstrate their professional experience with both past and present employers. Colleagues and clients can recommend you by writing testimonials. As such, it's a great place to further enhance your personal brand and your reputation on social media.

As with many social networks, you could spend a lot of time adding bells and whistles to your profile. Beyond descriptions of your experience you can add portfolios, presentations, blogs, and more. To begin, just provide the basic information: experience, education, and your personal summary. As you have time, build out deeper descriptions throughout your profile. Write recommendations for other users. And don't be afraid to ask other users to make introductions or write recommendations for you, too!

Once you have the basics of your profile set up, be sure your firm has a profile as well. Here you can add firm-wide information and link to all your employees who are also on the network. As a side note, be sure all of your employees are linking to the correct company on LinkedIn. Sometimes the system will allow you to add the name of your employer without requiring the company's profile to be connected to it. This can get confusing when you pull up your company page, but not everyone is listed.

Lastly, LinkedIn offers premium features for paid users, including deeper analytics, job postings, and more. Although premium features can be very useful for some users, most seem to do very well with the "basic" free account.

Is Facebook "professional enough" for your firm?

In the case of Facebook, it's hard to argue with the numbers. Just about everyone with an Internet connection has a Facebook profile, and the number of users grows larger each day.

Even so, many of our clients have expressed misgivings about using Facebook to market their professional firm. It's not a position that I would quickly disagree with. However, I think you should consider each social network, and what your purpose would be for being on that particular network.

Many of our clients have individual Facebook pages set aside for personal friends and family. If they determine to "friend" a client, it's usually someone they've known outside of the typical client relationship. We're not talking about using your personal Facebook page to market per se. What we are talking about is having a company or brand page that your friends, family, business partners, vendors, and clients can "like." And when you "like" a page, your company's info may begin to start showing up in your friends' streams. It's just one more way to spread the word about your firm.

We recommend keeping the sales and marketing language light on Facebook. Make posts that celebrate victories, milestones, or team-building activities, and/or posts that show a more personal side to your firm. Your page is also a great place for your current employees to share with each other, especially if your firm is spread out across multiple offices. Over time, you may even find that your Facebook page is a better recruitment tool or referral source than methods you've used in the past.

As with LinkedIn, a free account will probably suffice. However, Facebook does provide opportunities for extremely targeted advertising within its network, even outside of your friends and fans. If you only want to advertise to female grads of Purdue University from 1999 who listen to the Indigo Girls, you can do that. Traditionally, these Facebook ads are on a pay-per-click model, so your firm only pays when someone clicks through on your ad.

Is advertising on Facebook right for every professional services firm? Absolutely not. You'll have to discuss this within your organization to figure out the best approach. It's hard to say if your clients would ever "buy" from you on Facebook, but one thing's for sure: they're probably already on Facebook.

To tweet or not to tweet.

Are you leery about using Twitter? It's a common feeling among many professionals. And yet some professionals, attorneys in particular, are now flocking to this 140-character-limited social network.

I think the common feeling among non-Twitter users is that

everyone on Twitter is an egomaniac, posting (i.e., tweeting) some mix of what they had for lunch, which famous people they know, or how smart they are. While not everyone on Twitter behaves this way, the network has its fair share of egos. Of course, that doesn't mean you have to be one of them.

The reality is that Twitter, like LinkedIn and Facebook, can provide great opportunities to connect with like-minded people, create top-of-mind awareness of your firm, reinforce your firm's areas of expertise, and even attract top talent.

So how do you get started?

1. Choose your handle.

Visit Twitter.com to select your handle. Pick something like your name or your company's name. This handle will be your Twitter username, and your posts will show up with "@" in front of them. You've probably seen this before in print ads or TV commercials. I'm @joshmiles. You may find that your name or company name is already taken, so get creative. You'll also want to upload your photo and customize your profile page.

Add your handle as another piece of contact information on your email signature, e-newsletter, blog, and website. If it makes sense, consider adding it to your print materials (e.g., business cards) and/or sharing it in articles, during presentations, and at networking events.

2. Share good stuff.

One obvious use for Twitter is to share your firm's ideas, links, and articles. First of all, write posts worth reading. In general, stick to what you know. This doesn't mean you have to be robotic, but if you're tweeting more about sushi than your area of expertise, some of your professional followers may lose interest.

Just remember this on Twitter: aim to share, not sell. Users follow people for various reasons, but few will continue to follow users who post blatant sales messages.

Say things worth repeating. If someone reposts what you write, it's called a retweet, or RT. If you want to share what someone else has posted, you can retweet their post as well. When you do so, the RT in front of their post shows you are retweeting them. When someone retweets your message, it goes to all of that person's followers, which is a great way for more people to be exposed to you.

If you have something private to tweet to another user, you can send a direct message (these start with a "D"). You can also have direct messages sent to your mobile phone as text messages.

3. Grow your influence.

How do you become an influential Twitter user? Start by following interesting people, or anyone you like for that matter. Retweet good stuff. Be polite. When users tweet "@" you, tweet back.

Stay on top of your account. Keep an eye on who's following you, and choose who makes sense to follow in return (just because someone follows you does not mean you have to reciprocate). Find other users who talk about similar keywords and consider following them as well. Clients, vendors, co-workers, and even other experts are great people to follow.

Use Twitter to provide tips, link to informative articles, make announcements, share news, promote awards, and more. Don't limit your thinking to what you can fit in 140 characters or less. You can link to longer content such as websites, videos, and blogs, too. Speaking of blogs, every posting at your firm would be greatly complemented by a Twitter mention or two, wouldn't it?

A Flickr Gallery That Fueled $2 Million in Sales

TKO Graphics is an Indianapolis-based, large-format graphics company specializing in vehicle wraps and nationwide installation. They recently secured their largest client in company history by using Flickr and social media as part of their marketing mix.

To date TKO has installed more than 4,000 vehicles in more than 200 locations for this client—to the tune of nearly $2 million. How did they do it?

As TKO Director of Communications Randy Clark will quickly tell you, social media wasn't the only piece to this sale, but it was the catalyst.

TKO's marketing department regularly updates the company's portfolio across a variety of social media tools. This particular lead came from the company's Flickr feed, which introduced their capabilities to another vehicle graphics company, Moore and More, in St. Louis.

From there, TKO met with Moore and More to see how they could collaborate. The eventual outcome was a referral to an ad agency that helped TKO land the nationwide vehicle graphics installation project.

So while social media produced the opportunity, TKO's good old fashioned, face-to-face networking is what turned the opportunity into a $2 million sale.

"So, when someone tells you social media doesn't work, tell 'em about our 6,000 vehicle contract—unless it's our competitors, then tell 'em it doesn't work," Randy jokes.

Randy would also tell you that while social media marketing is great, it's only part of the picture. "When someone says 'I'm only doing social marketing, and dropping everything else,' I'd caution them not to quit everything else they've been doing. Social media can bring leads—but it's still up to you to close the sale."

It may be helpful to think of Twitter like my friend Lorraine Ball (@LorraineBall) says, "Twitter is like one big cocktail party. If you wouldn't say it at a party, don't post it on Twitter."

4. But don't stop there.

There are many more things you can do with Twitter. Tweeting functionality is built into various websites, smartphones, and desktop applications. One of my favorite Twitter clients is a free website called TweetDeck.com, which has a companion desktop and mobile app.

TweetDeck enables you to manage multiple Twitter accounts, view groups, shorten links, and post photos; it even provides support for other social networks such as Facebook and LinkedIn. If TweetDeck isn't cutting it for you, take a look at HootSuite, CoTweet, or one of the many iPhone, iPad, and Android apps built especially for tweeting.

Get into the habit of making regular updates. Choose specific days or times of the day to spend quality time on Twitter. It could be five minutes or five hours a day, depending on how Twitter best fits into your overall communications strategy.

Some Twitter clients will allow you to schedule future Twitter posts. This isn't always the best idea, but it may be a good tactic for you to better utilize your time on social media.

You can also use hashtags within your tweets. This means that you "tag" your post with the pound sign, such as #branding. Hashtags enable other users to track tweets around specific topics. They're also popular at conferences and other events.

Commit some time to discussing your goals and strategies before jumping right in with Twitter, but don't sit back for too long. Being an active Twitter user may be one of the best ways to position your brand as an expert firm and generate new leads.

And don't forget to have a little fun. If used in good balance, Twitter is a great way to showcase some of your firm's culture as well as some of your personal interests.

Video: Putting stories in motion.

If you're like most professionals I've met, you're probably not thrilled by the thought of making videos of yourself for the entire world to see. Unfortunately for you, this book is about branding and marketing...so you're going to have to get over yourself and do some video. Just kidding! Well, sort of.

"Contrary to what most people might think after meeting me in business, or hearing me do a speech, I'm actually shy," says Scott Abbott, entrepreneur, social investor, and author of Pocket PorchLights. "Frankly, I'm an introvert; I'm not hungry to put myself out there. That said, I consider it my personal, fiduciary responsibility to speak up, and publicly represent our companies' activities and social interests. It takes some getting used to, and I don't always enjoy it. But it's the right thing to do. After all, it's not about me: it's about those I serve. That's what servant leadership, is all about."

Online B2B video is growing at a breakneck pace. And it's not just YouTube anymore (although that's still the largest video aggregation site in the world). Many social networks have options for online video. Vimeo, Facebook, LinkedIn, and even SlideShare are in on the video game.

So, why video? Frankly, some people would rather watch a 60-second video than read a few paragraphs. And perhaps more accurately, video gives your prospective clients an opportunity to experience "you" without ever meeting face-to-face, or even picking up the phone.

Video (if used well) is a great way to demonstrate your thinking, show off your office, introduce your team, or even show your people in action—literally.

But I'm not a fan of just any video.

I hate boring "talking head" videos that reveal messy offices and disheveled appearances. It also irritates me when videos take six minutes to tell a two-minute story. And finally, when the video's content screams, "It's all about me," I feel a little sorry for the company and their audience.

Amateur video isn't always a bad thing, but bad amateur video—or what I call "professionally bad"—is what bugs me. Goofy graphics. Bad green screen people superimposed over a silly backdrop image. Awkward edits...if Wayne and Garth could have done it better on public access, maybe video just isn't your thing.

On the other hand, amateur video can work on many levels. Self-shot videos of you talking to your iPhone or Flip camera on a job site, or on your "live blog," are in fact, very cool. They help your audience feel like they're experiencing the authentic you. It feels real and human. It doesn't have to come off flawlessly to be successful.

I love video when it takes me places or tells a great story. I love testimonial videos, especially when they're showing me something more than what I can read on your website. Give me human interaction and show me someone I can relate to. Someone I can trust. This is online video I can get behind.

So maybe video isn't a fit for everyone, but don't discount it just because it's different. Nothing portrays humans like...well, humans talking to us on video.

Keeping score.

How many friends, followers, fans, or Klout points do you need to feel successful?

Of course, that's a trick question. In the end, your numbers are just that. Numbers. It might be nice for a right-brained office environment to track its social stats, but stats alone won't yield sales.

In reality, you may find value in tracking the number of your followers, tweets, friends, fans, or connections. It may help you determine which social networks are showing positive growth, but that alone isn't enough.

Then there are those who only want to talk about "engagement" and "joining in the conversation." These terms are warm and fuzzy enough, but they drive analytical types crazy. How in the heck do you measure engagement?

Some websites, such as Klout, actually attempt to measure social influence by analyzing some combination of activity and responses to your postings.

In the end, the things you should be tracking are the things that drove you to use social media in the first place. If you're using social media to generate "new leads," track which leads have originated from, or have been nurtured by, social media. If a goal was to improve recruitment, find a way to score the quality of talent you find on social media versus other channels.

After all, if you don't track your social media activities in ways that are valuable to your firm, how can anyone else help you determine what to do?

But wait, there's more.

So are LinkedIn, Facebook, Twitter, and YouTube the only social sites your firm should consider? Of course not. In addition to these, be sure to consider Google+, Quora, Foursquare, and photo-sharing applications like Pinterest, Flickr, and Instagram. The point is you'll probably want to at least explore the major social networks, but go ahead and scope out the others, too.

Does your firm need a social media policy?

Social media policies have been a hot topic for many businesses lately. Surely you've seen news stories about employees being terminated for their social media activity, former employees being sued to recover their Twitter accounts and their followers, or even disclaimers in bios featured in social media profiles. Social media policies are becoming increasingly more common, and are definitely worth considering for your firm.

I'm certainly no HR or legal expert, but my advice is this: If your firm allows or requires employees to participate in social media, having a simple, straightforward social media policy is a wise move. It's a good opportunity to spell out what is expected, what is allowable, and what activities (if any) might jeopardize an employee's good standing within the firm.

Kyle Lacy, author of *Twitter Marketing for Dummies* and *Branding Yourself*, points out that having a social media policy is not enough—you also have to train your people on using it.

"If you aren't making expectations clear, it's really unfair to your employees," Kyle says. "Not having a written, communicated social networking policy is like being without HR policies."

Here's what works for me.

Don't you love it when someone gives you a bunch of new things you're supposed to learn? I may be a bit cynical, but I always wondered how much my past "teachers" were taking their own advice.

To that point, I'd like to share with you how I use my time on social media, and what has worked for our firm. Will this work for you? No guarantees there. In the end, you'll have to make your own way, but here's a peek inside my social activity.

I make the social networks work for me. I don't have a ton of time every day to commit to social media.

I have "active" accounts on Facebook, Twitter, and LinkedIn. Others too, but those are my core accounts. I use TweetDeck to monitor my @MilesDesign and @JoshMiles accounts. I also post to Twitter, Facebook, and LinkedIn directly from TweetDeck. Many professionals I know comment on my frequent activity on LinkedIn, but here's my super secret: Every time I post to Twitter it automatically posts the same content to LinkedIn. I seldom get on LinkedIn just to hang out.

On average, I commit 30 minutes each weekday on social media. Sometimes it's zero, and sometimes it's much more, it just depends on the day.

I use social media to learn about what our clients are talking about, find new talent, stay inspired, learn about new things, and keep up with my friends all over the country. In the end, it's a lot of fun, too. Social media is not our greatest lead source, but it's definitely growing. We've received leads from all over the country from our activity across various sites, and I've definitely noticed a correlation between social media and top-of-mind awareness.

The bottom line? Even with minimal daily effort, it's a valuable use of my time. And if you commit to it for the right reasons, I think you'll agree. It's not as intimidating as you may have thought.

Homework:

☐ Think about why you want to be active on social media.

☐ Look at your overall business strategy to determine which social networks might be most beneficial to your firm.

☐ Develop a social media strategy. Use it to help determine which activities you want to concentrate on and what stats you want to track.

☐ Rethink social media outlets you haven't considered in the past (e.g., Twitter and YouTube).

☐ Have you discovered any niche social networks that have been surprisingly beneficial?

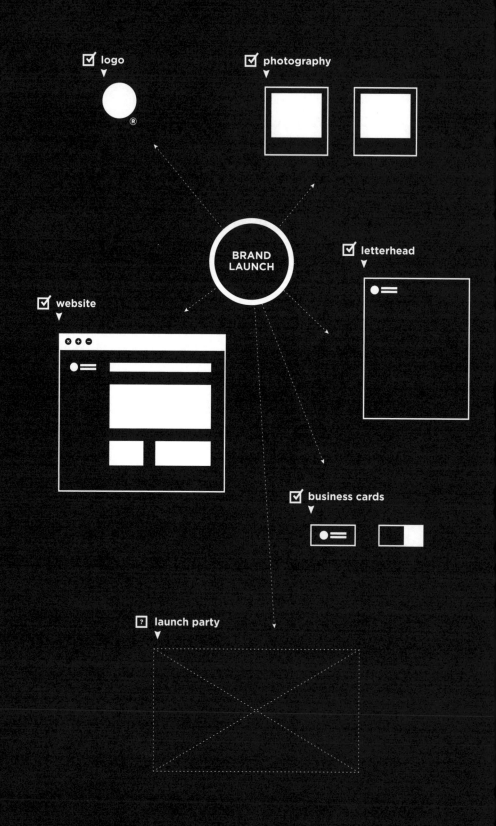

CHAPTER THIRTEEN

Internal Culture & Rollout of Your Bold Brand

One of the most often overlooked elements of a branding exercise is, without a doubt, the internal brand launch.

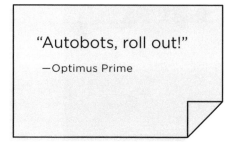

"Autobots, roll out!"

—Optimus Prime

What happens when it's go time?

Let's think back here. Do you remember why most professional services firms find it so important to rebrand in the first place?

• Undergoing a merger or acquisition?

• Shifting your approach or business model?

• Hoping to shed excess baggage or negative PR?

• Need to better position yourself in the market?

• Or maybe you simply need to update your look and refresh your brand?

Without a doubt, the most successful branding exercises not only address the problems above, but also serve as a compass for your firm's brand.

The goal is to guarantee that everyone in your firm is now speaking the same language and singing from the same hymnal. Remember, branding goes far, far beyond the marketing campaigns you launch, or sales meetings you host. Everyone in your firm contributes to the brand that your clients will experience.

Even human resources-related problems, such as poor morale, inconsistent management, or a lack of systems, will guide how a professional services firm fully expresses its brand to the world.

So regardless of how much time, money, or effort you have spent on your rebranding effort, your team's willingness (or lack thereof) to participate at this new level, and to reflect your new brand, will have a direct impact on the success of your rebranding effort.

Therefore, it's essential that your entire firm understands what your new brand is about, and why it's so important to live the brand internally and externally. When your firm members are out and about in the market, everything they do—the way they approach situations, treat people, and simply conduct business—must consistently reflect what your brand stands for.

Without a doubt, your team needs to walk the talk. But they aren't going to be able to walk the talk until they buy into, and fully understand, what the "talk" is all about.

The best way to get everyone in your organization on the same page regarding your new brand is to get everyone involved and aware of what is happening and why this rebrand is taking place. This doesn't mean you need to take every employee's feedback into account during the rebrand, but don't let something as extensive as a firm-wide rebrand come as a complete surprise, especially to key staff and client-facing team members.

Throw a Brand Launch Party.

So assuming you're not just going to throw a "surprise party" to let everyone know about the rebrand, a party probably is the right mindset for this announcement. Choose a time and place where you can have your entire team in the same room to announce it. A branding rollout meeting should feel like a celebration, so why not make your brand launch an actual party?

The goal of the party is to rally the troops around your rebranding efforts. You want to create excitement and buzz internally, which in turn will spill over externally. As with any good party, plan to have entertainment, music, food, and drinks. Map out your agenda and schedule the party at the end of a work week.

The party doesn't have to be overly expensive. You can host it in your offices, but special occasions call for a change of pace. How about holding it at a hotel? Or the back room of a steakhouse? Or even at an outdoor park? It's really more about what fits your brand and corporate culture and less about how much the party costs.

Let's be clear. This party isn't just to have a good time. It's to boldly carve out a new direction for your company and your brand. After your team has had a chance to eat a few Swedish meatballs, it's time to show them what you've been working on.

To get your message across clearly, you have three choices: hand out a brand manual, show a video, or get up on stage and speak.

Speaking is the least expensive option, but it can be pretty nerve racking. It doesn't matter if you're a great speaker or not, as long as you hit the high points. If you're unsure of where to go with your speech, here are a few recommendations:

Extend a warm welcome. Let everyone roll in on a relaxed note with music playing and food being served. Even if there are only a handful of employees, make everyone feel like a "guest."

Be enthusiastic. If you're not visibly excited about your new brand, how can you expect your team to be?

Keep it brief. Nobody wants to stop enjoying themselves for too long, so get to the point!

Start with a story. Tell them about how you first envisioned the brand, or what you see in the future, and how this will help all of you get there faster.

Don't dwell on the past. This isn't the time or place to say how awful the company's public perception has been up until this point, or to be down on the brand's recent past. But you can talk about what you saw as opportunities, and why now was the best time to make a move.

Convey the brand essence. Hit the high points and emphasize the most compelling elements of the new brand.

Show and tell. There's nothing quite like showing off your new toys—whatever you have that's visual at this point will make for some great "oohs and aahs." Before-and-after comparisons are nice as well.

Encourage everyone to live the brand. Lastly, remind your guests how important each and every one of them is to your company. Tell them how much you need them to live the brand both internally and externally. Reassure them that they'll be hearing more in the coming weeks, and give them a point person within your company to contact with any questions.

After your speech:

Distribute the schwag. Once you've accepted the thunderous applause, pass out items emblazoned with your new identity. I've seen small companies hand out branded iPods, and larger companies distribute branded t-shirts or hats. Regardless of the value of the item, wrapping up the event by passing out a fun item can be an incredibly valuable next move.

Let it live on. Sometimes the announcements, invitations, or press releases for your brand launch are even more important to the buzz of your launch than the event itself. If you're comfortable making this a public event, be sure to hit up the right media outlets before and after the launch. Provide them with a high-resolution logo, and maybe even images of your new website and collateral.

Publicize and follow up on your launch on social media as well. Use tools like your blog and YouTube to generate buzz.

Distributing communications documents.

Of course, the "more information" your team will receive as the weeks roll on might include a revised HR manual, updated policies, and "brand standards" spelling out some do's and don'ts. But will everyone in your company need a copy of your detailed brand standards manual or communication protocols? That's doubtful, but you may want to consider a "lighter" version that outlines the new identity without getting too deeply into the marketing details.

Avoid the temptation to appear "overly corporate" with your first follow up. Send out a thank you for attending the brand launch event or a link to photos from the party. The most important thing is that this next communication carries on your new look and the new brand voice.

Moving forward, you may want to give each employee a custom-designed and branded internal documentation binder (you can find these at sites like NakedBinder.com or Paolocardelli.com). As you issue future documentation, each piece can be put into the binder.

Initial documents to put into the binder might include:

- Mission statement

- Vision statement

- Statement of your values and corporate culture

- Sample elevator pitch

- Email signature standards

- Telephone and voice mail standards

- Logo, tagline, and basic brand vocabulary

Follow-up documents might address:

- Social media policy

- HR basics

- Corporate policies and procedures

- Customer service expectations and beliefs

- Sales process/customer relationship management

It isn't necessary for every sticky note or memo to be overtly branded, but remember, every touch point of your brand is an opportunity to build your brand equity, tear it down, or have no effect. Be intentional about each touch point and consider its impact. You never know who might see your branded e-memo, spoken in your unique voice, expressing the special flavor of your brand and culture!

Homework:

☐ What type of launch event would best fit with your firm's culture? An internal pep rally? A cocktail party?

☐ Throw a party for employees and clients.

☐ Launch a media campaign to publicize your new brand.

☐ Follow up with employees by providing guidelines for internal communications.

CHAPTER FOURTEEN

Keeping Your Professional Brand Fresh

How to keep the excitement alive.

> "Can we do something else to make it pop?"
>
> —Every client in the history of marketing

If I had a nickel for every client who got a little bored at some point with having a consistent brand, I'd have a lot of nickels.

Maybe you've thought it before about your brand.

Have you ever said:

"We really need to add some more sizzle to our website."

"What can we do to spruce this up?"

"Let's do something different with this one!"

The exciting part of developing a new brand is that everything is new. The downside is that once many companies experience the thrill of newness, conforming to the brand standards can seem, well, somewhat dull.

So how can you, as "keeper of the brand," maintain a level of excitement, while still delivering a consistent brand?

One guaranteed way to keep your brand fresh is to host an annual, semi-annual, or quarterly client event. It's a great way to share the latest and greatest about your company with your employees, clients, and prospects. Not to mention, it's a powerful incentive to keep your marketing team on their toes. Obviously, throwing a huge conference is a major undertaking. Your first event doesn't have to feature a Fortune 100 CEO or a Top-40 musical act. Scale your event to fit where your brand is today.

Even if all you ever plan to host is a cocktail party, attending well-respected conferences is a fantastic way to find inspiration for your future events.

What if your Bold Brand starts to feel stale?

Before you rush to revisit the brand, take a closer look at your brand standards manual.

Your brand standards should provide plenty of freedom to create exciting pieces while offering ample safety from doing something totally off-brand. And before you go tweaking what you've just finished, keep in mind that the only people getting bored with the consistency of your brand are probably your own team members. But you know what? Consistency and individuality were some of the most important reasons for creating this whole brand thing in the first place, remember?

When your brand goes through rough waters, it's often more of a people management issue. Sometimes it's just a matter of keeping your team aware of what the brand is doing visually. This doesn't mean that everyone should get a vote on every design element, color, or campaign. The complete opposite is actually true. But communicating with the team is usually enough to 1) keep everyone on-board with your brand, and 2) keep internal boredom or dissatisfaction with your marketing materials at bay.

Sometimes it helps to point to consumer brands to convey the importance of brand consistency. Ask your team to list some of their favorite retail brands, and then ask them how often these brands completely change it up. If they're being honest, they'll realize that while campaigns may come and go, successful brands as a whole are more often than not very consistent.

If you're considering trying something new for your next campaign, look at your brand standards as the ballpark that you need to play within. Then find the boundaries of just how far you CAN push your brand's visual elements within those standards.

ExactTarget: *Connections*

ExactTarget, a provider of cross-channel interactive marketing solutions, hosts thousands of interactive marketers in Indianapolis each year at its annual Connections conference.

Tim Kopp, ExactTarget's chief marketing officer, is incredibly passionate about the Connections event: "We believe in delivering value to our attendees through top-notch industry content, inspiring and motivating keynote speakers, and assiduous attention to detail."

And with a speaker roster that has included the likes of Sir Richard Branson, Malcolm Gladwell, and Soledad O'Brien, ExactTarget's passion for delivering value is clearly more than lipservice.

"For the last five years, ExactTarget has invited its ecosystem of clients, partners, prospects, analysts, and employees to Indianapolis to be inspired, educated, and entertained," Tim explains. "The experience gives attendees a true taste of the ExactTarget brand—from hearing the company vision from executives on the main stage, to the educational breakout sessions presented by clients and ExactTarget employees, to the attention to detail at every interaction from the moment you arrive in Indianapolis."

As any professional services salesperson will tell you, the benefits of engaging your clients and prospects on a deeper level beyond a sales environment can be invaluable. "That's why we believe hosting a successful user conference can be one of the best ways to do just that. To us, it's all about the attendee experience," Tim adds.

And it's not just ExactTarget's word. Having been an attendee, I can attest to the power and professionalism of this event.

And although I could probably write another chapter with nothing but testimonials from past Connections events, I think this one sums it up pretty well: "We attend events all the time and...we take note of whether the hosting entity takes care of the details the way that we would. Without a doubt, this is one of the most well-executed events we've ever attended."

Aside from glowing reviews, how does ExactTarget gauge the impact of the event? By using a tool called the Net Promoter Score (NPS) to measure the likelihood of an attendee recommending the conference.

> As Tim shares, "Through a focused strategy on the attendee experience we have been able to increase our Net Promoter Score for the past three years. Our last Connections event scored nearly twice as high as the average user conference in our industry. NPS is a great way for us to understand how successful our conference has been at delivering value to the attendee."

Even more impressive than the stats is the fan-like affinity that I witnessed firsthand as a Connections attendee. This is definitely an event that reinforces the energy and personality of the ExactTarget brand.

Does this mean you can't ever cross the lines? Of course not. There should always be room for improvement. If you find your brand standards to be overly confining, here are a few areas you can experiment with:

Logo usage. Experimenting with your logo is probably the best place to begin. Sometimes just trying an alternate logo presentation, such as reversing it out of your marketing materials (making the logo white on a field of color, pattern, or photographic background) can be a striking refresh. If your brand standards were professionally designed, chances are logo usage isn't the best element of your standards to tweak, but if a reverse-out logo wasn't originally used, give it a try.

Color palette. This is a good place to look next. Do you have any complementary colors selected for your brand standards? Having a few other colors to play off of in your marketing materials can really open up the possibilities of what your brand can do visually. Is your color palette too loud? Try introducing a muted color set. And if it's feeling a little too dry, try a few pops of more intense color. Check out sites like Kuler.com if you want some inspiration.

Alternate typography. If your materials are only using one type family, choosing a complementary typeface or two can be another great way to add some variety to your brand. The first elements to consider new type options for are headlines, body text, and other callouts. At first pass, don't mess with the fonts in the logo, tagline, or other standard lock-ups.

Custom photography. A picture may be worth 1,000 words, but if you're using the same old stock images as your competitors, it's no wonder you've lost the passion for your brand. Commercial photographers are fantastic to collaborate with. The mood, theme, or lighting of your photography is an exciting element to play with to freshen up the look of everything your brand touches.

In the end, being "bored with brand consistency" isn't really the best reason to update your brand. But what are some legitimate reasons why a company should look for a refresh?

The biggest reason we see is growth; however, just growing larger than you were isn't usually the lone impetus. More often, growth presents itself as moving your headquarters, adding a new location, bringing in new business partners, acquiring another firm, or adding key staff.

The second biggest reason is a change of focus. Maybe you've added new services, moved into a new market space, or simply need to better carve out your positioning.

Does all of this feel like the setup for an all-out rebrand? No— don't have a panic attack! This framework doesn't feed on itself. The goal isn't to always be in a state of rebranding. Your goal should be to keep the brand up-to-date, unique, and appropriate to who your firm is.

This means that the more thorough a job you've done on your positioning and brand standards, the more longevity you should get from that work—and the less work you'll need to do the next time around. So instead of starting from scratch, you'll be standing on the shoulders of where your brand has already grown.

What's next for your firm?

Before you get started, spend some time in the following pages with our DIY Bold Brand Audit. Imagine your brand sometime in the future. What assets, tools, collateral, and stories would you like to have? What do you have now, and what is missing?

How can you bridge the gap to where that ideal brand stands in the future?

To get there, you'll need buy-in from your company's leaders, and you may want to consider working with a brand strategy specialist.

It's important to find a branding firm that specializes in your area of expertise. Interview several, but don't expect any to work for free. Reputable firms bill either as a fixed fee, or on a time-and-materials basis, but shouldn't offer to do any speculative work without being compensated.

As you consider your needs, think about them like a brand strategist would. Managing and maintaining your Bold Brand should be an ongoing activity, not a one-time event.

Building your professional services brand within our Bold Brand framework isn't easy. It requires you to dig deep and make serious strategic business decisions about who you are—and who you want to be as a brand. And most importantly, this framework provides a proven process for you and your collaborators to build a great professional services brand, from the ground up.

Homework:

☐ How can you help keep your brand interesting?

☐ What type of annual, semi-annual, or quarterly event can your firm host?

☐ How can you do something fresh, without completely tossing out your brand standards?

☐ What would new photography do for your brand?

☐ How could an alternate color palette help add a spark to your brand identity?

WHO ARE YOU?
DIY Brand Checklist

- [X] Voice and Style
- [X] Visual identity
- [X] Collateral
- [X] Website
- [X] Social Media
- [X] Other brand exposures

Branded

CHAPTER FIFTEEN

DIY Bold Brand Audit

How can you tell if your brand is due for an overhaul without spending a lot of money on a branding consultant?

What is your elevator pitch?

Ask yourself the following:

Positioning

- Who are you?

- What is your market?

- What is your product or service?

- What is your Unique Selling Proposition (USP)?

- What is your brand essence?

- What are your brand values?

- Describe your corporate culture. Does it fit your brand?

- What is your elevator speech? Mission? Vision?

- Would everyone in your company describe your brand similarly?

- Are important decision-makers aware of your branding and marketing initiatives?

Voice and Style

- Describe your brand voice.

- Review sample headlines.

- Review sample copy.

- Review usage—how do you use your company or brand name in the following: possessive, plural, product, service, in combination with other items, etc.

- How do you write your company name? All caps, title case, shorthand, something else?

Visual identity

- Is your name trademarked or registered?

- Do you have a single logo or trademark?

- Is it used consistently across your materials?

Collateral

- Round up samples of your materials—brochures, print materials, tradeshow displays, advertising, etc.

- Do they look like they're from the same company?

- Are any of them outdated, or formatted in an inappropriate style?

- Is your brand used consistently, following a standard set of rules?

- Are the colors consistent across various pieces?

Website

- Search performance—can you be found online when you search for your name, or your product/service?

Social Media

- Are your social media sites up to date? Do they accurately reflect your brand?

Other brand exposures

Check all that apply to your company or brand:

- Sponsorships/civic involvement/memberships

- News/PR

- External assets—speaking engagements, articles, books, blogs, etc.

- Testimonials

- Videos

- HR policies/on-boarding process

- Internal systems

- Customer service

- Internal surveys

- Client surveys

Envision the future state of your professional brand

- What does your brand currently look like?

- What types of assets, tools, collateral, or stories do you want to have?

- Which of these pieces do you have now, and which are missing?

- What are the first priorities for reaching your future state?

Homework:

☐ Review the results of your DIY Bold Brand Audit.

☐ Who else needs to see this?

☐ Rally your team and leadership to plan for the next steps.

☐ Does your in-house team have the expertise to accomplish your goals? Or will you need to interview branding consultants to help build your brand?

☐ Hire the team that best fits your personality, goals, budget, and timeline.

To download a PDF copy of the DIY Bold Brand Audit checklist, visit: www.boldbrand.com/book/downloads

About Bold Brand™

Bold Brand™ is a framework and best-practices approach to help professional services firms identify a niche, position themselves within that niche, and build a compelling brand. This framework guides professionals step-by-step through the process, illuminating potential pitfalls along the way.

Bold Brand™ is the process we've built our branding practice on at Miles Design. It's a process and framework that applies to a broad cross-section of professional services and B2B clients.

Visit BoldBrand.com for additional resources, and to download the DIY Bold Brand Audit checklist.

About Josh Miles

Josh Miles is the principal and founder of Miles Design, an Indianapolis-based, award-winning design firm specializing in brand strategy, corporate identity, and website design for professional services firms. Josh's expertise is highly sought after by organizations including architects, attorneys, engineers, consultants, and software companies.

Prior to starting Miles Design, Josh served as an art director and an adjunct faculty member for three university-level graphic design programs. Josh is a long-time member of AIGA, the professional association for design, having served three years as the Indianapolis chapter president. Josh is currently involved in the American Institute of Architects (AIA), the Society for Marketing Professional Services (SMPS), and Rainmakers, a B2B professional networking organization. Josh also serves on the board of Oasis Network for Churches (OasNet), an international church planting and resourcing organization for churches spreading the gospel of God's grace.

Josh is addicted to problem solving, coffee, and progress.

Josh is a partner in several other startup and technology-related companies in Indianapolis.

Josh lives in Indianapolis with his beautiful wife, daughter, and newborn son.

For more information, or to book Josh as a speaker, please visit:
- JoshMiles.com
- BoldBrand.com
- MilesDesign.com
- Twitter.com/JoshMiles

You may also reach Josh via:
- josh@milesdesign.com
- 317.915.8693

Resources

Books mentioned in Bold Brand:

- Abbott, Scott. *Pocket PorchLights.* AuthorHouse, 2008.

- Deckers, Erik and Lacy, Kyle. *Branding Yourself: How to Use Social Media to Invent or Reinvent Yourself.* Que Biz-Tech, 2011.

- Enns, Blair. *The Win Without Pitching Manifesto.* RockBench Publishing Corp., 2010.

- Fried, Jason and Heinemeier Hansson, David. *Rework.* Crown Business, 2010.

- Gladwell, Malcolm. *Outliers: The Story of Success.* Little, Brown and Company, 2008.

- Heath, Chip and Heath, Dan. *Switch: How to Change Things When Change Is Hard.* Crown Publishing Group, 2010.

- Hogshead, Sally. *Fascinate: Your 7 Triggers to Persuasion and Captivation.* HarperCollins Publishers, 2010.

- Lacy, Kyle. *Twitter Marketing For Dummies.* Wiley Publishing, Inc., 2010.

- McKain, Scott. *Collapse of Distinction: Stand out and move up while your competition fails.* Thomas Nelson, 2009.

- Neumeier, Marty. *The Brand Gap: How to Bridge the Distance Between Business Strategy and Design.* New Riders Press, 2003.

- Pulizzi, Joe and Barrett, Newt. *Get Content Get Customers: Turn Prospects into Buyers with Content Marketing.* McGraw-Hill, 2009.

Interested in learning more about content marketing?

- Visit ContentMarketingInstitute.com for an extensive collection of content marketing resources, including information about Content Marketing World.

- Check out Eloqua.com and search for the *Grande Guide to B2B Content Marketing.*

- Visit ContentMarketingToday.com for content marketing information in an integrated website and blog.

Organizations and websites mentioned in Bold Brand:

- AIA.org

- AIGA.org

- B2BBloggers.com

- Compendium.com

- Connections2012.com

- ContentMarketingInstitute.com

- ContentMarketingWorld.com

- ContentMarketingInstitute.com/blog/

- Enquiro.com

- ExactTarget.com

- Hubspot.com

- KennedyVanDerLaan.com

- Klout.com

- KyleLacy.com

- LorraineBall.com

- LucasMiles.Wordpress.com

- MarketingProfs.com

- MarketingTechBlog.com

- MarkZweig.com

- MilesDesign.com

- MyEmma.com

- OHM-Advisors.com

- RatioArchitects.com

- SallyHogshead.com

- ScottMcKain.com

- SMPS.org

- TKOGraphix.com

- WinWithoutPitching.com

- ZweigWhite.com

Acknowledgments

A huge thank you to Mark Zweig.

Thank you to my family, friends, our Indianapolis network, and beyond—AIGA, Rainmakers, SMPS, and everyone featured in this book—for your love, help, and encouragement.

Thank you to CJ McClanahan for making a crazy bet, and always holding me accountable to my goals.

Thank you to Joe Pulizzi, Newt Barrett, Lisa Beets, and the entire team at Content Marketing Institute for making this a reality.

Thank you to the entire team at Miles Design for your support throughout this process. You made this possible.

Typeface: Gotham by Hoefler & Frere-Jones
http://www.typography.com/

Cover photography and headshot: Studio Thirteen
http://www.studio13online.com/

Book design: Miles Design
Layout: Brian K Gray
Illustrations: Jon McClure